Material Phenomenology

Series Board

James Bernauer

Drucilla Cornell

Thomas R. Flynn

Kevin Hart

Richard Kearney

Jean-Luc Marion

Adriaan Peperzak

Thomas Sheehan

Hent de Vries

Merold Westphal

Edith Wyschogrod

Michael Zimmerman

John D. Caputo, *series editor*

Perspectives in
Continental
Philosophy

MICHEL HENRY

Material Phenomenology

Translated by Scott Davidson

Fordham University Press
New York ■ 2008

Copyright © 2008 Fordham University Press

All rights reserved. No part of this publication may be reproduced, stored in a retrieval system, or transmitted in any form or by any means—electronic, mechanical, photocopy, recording, or any other—except for brief quotations in printed reviews, without the prior permission of the publisher.

Material Phenomenology was originally published in French as Michel Henry, *Phénoménologie Matérielle*, © Presses Universitaires de France, 1990.

Library of Congress Cataloging-in-Publication Data is available from the publisher.

10 09   5 4 3 2
First edition

Contents

	Translator's Preface	*ix*
	List of Abbreviations	*xvii*
	Introduction: The Question of Phenomenology	*1*
1.	Hyletic Phenomenology and Material Phenomenology	7
2.	The Phenomenological Method	43
3.	Pathos-With	
	Reflections on Husserl's Fifth Cartesian Meditation	*101*
	For a Phenomenology of Community	*118*
	Notes	*135*

Translator's Preface

Michel Henry (1922–2002) was a prolific French philosopher and novelist whose work sought to articulate a nonbiological concept of life. Indeed, Henry's understanding of life as a transcendental auto-affectivity is the guiding thread of his work from beginning to end. Over his career, he applied this understanding of life to a wide range of domains—including phenomenology, psychology, economics, politics, culture, art, music, and religion—in order to critique the devaluation of life wherever it may occur. Highly influential in France over the latter half of the twentieth century, his work remains underappreciated within the English-speaking world, in large part because of his antipathy to the passing Parisian fads and thus to the apparent "untimeliness" of his thought. To orient readers who may be encountering Henry's thought for the first time, in what follows I will situate *Material Phenomenology* within the broader context of his life and work.

Henry certainly would bristle at any insistence on the importance of the biographical details of his life, when his understanding of life refuses the equation of the self with anything that could be externalized in writing and recorded as a set of facts.[1] Indeed, when prompted to share his life story with an interviewer, Henry issued the following reply: "I would like to tell you how much I feel stripped away by the very idea of a biography. For one who thinks that the true self for us all is a non-worldly self, foreign to every empirical or objective determination, the attempt to approach him through these kinds of reference points seems to be problematic. The history of a man, the circumstances which surround him, are they anything other than a sort of mask, more or less flattering, that he and others agree to put on his face—he who, at bottom, has no face?"² Keeping in mind Henry's own reservations about the utility of biography, I nevertheless dare to offer some biographical information about his life, if only for the sake of helping the reader to gain easier access to this challenging body of work.

Henry was born in Haiphong, in what is now Vietnam, in 1922. His father died in an automobile accident when he was only seventeen days old. His mother, a concert pianist, was compelled shortly thereafter to return to her family home in Lille; later she moved to Paris. Henry's philosophical studies began at the Lycée Henri IV in Paris with a professor named René Bertrand. Although Henry's colleagues struggled to understand the abstract metaphysical texts they were assigned, he himself discovered an aptitude and passion for the world of ideas. He went on to pursue a course of study in philosophy at the university. His master's thesis, "Le Bonheur de Spinoza" (The Happiness of Spinoza), was completed in the winter of 1943 under the direction of Jean Grenier and became his first published work. Although Henry distances himself from Spinoza's metaphysical speculations therein, the influence of Spinoza is evident in Henry's later work through his continued commitment to a philosophy of immanence and, in particular, through his later reliance on Spinoza's notion of immanent causality to articulate the immanent structure of life.

During the summer of 1943, Henry followed the example of his older brother, who was a part of the Free French military stationed in England. He joined a Resistance group located in the Haut Jura and later operated in Lyon as an undercover agent. Fittingly, his codename was Kant, because *The Critique of Pure Reason* was the only item in his backpack when he joined up with the group. His wartime experience exerted a deep influence on his philosophy. Through his participation in the Resistance, Henry gained insight into the clandestine dimension of life. Unable either to say what he truly thought or to be who he truly was, Henry came to the realization in the Resistance that the true life is invisible. Drawing from this experience, Henry reminds us that each one of us always lives undercover, in a life essentially concealed from the visible masks donned in social and political life.

After completing his *agrégation* in 1945, Henry turned to Maine de Biran, the French philosopher of the body. In *Philosophy and Phenomenology of the Body*, which was initially intended to be a chapter of *The Essence of Manifestation*, Henry accepted de Biran's overcoming of Cartesian dualism through a more nuanced account of the body, but he went on to develop his own philosophical insights concerning the concrete immanence of the body.[3] Although this work was completed in 1949, it was not published in France until 1965. The reason for this was that doctoral defenses at that time required two theses to be published simultaneously, typically one that was historical and another that was original. The second thesis was to be his magnum opus, *The Essence of Manifestation* (1963).[4] Working over a span of ten years in almost complete isolation, Henry developed a rigorous critique of the German idealists Kant and Hegel, as well as their heirs in phenomenology, Husserl and Heidegger, showing that all of these thinkers, in spite of their apparent differences, were committed to a basic undercurrent of all Western thought: "ontological monism." Ontological monism, as Henry uses the term, refers to any view that reduces all being to one type of appearing, namely, that of transcendence. A distinguished dissertation committee, consisting of Jean Hyppolite, Jean Wahl, Paul Ricoeur, Ferdinand Alquié, and Henri Gouhier, accepted the thesis with high acclaim.

Eschewing repeated offers to teach in Paris at the Sorbonne, Henry preferred to lead a quiet, provincial life in which he could concentrate on his work without the distraction of Parisian intellectual life and the heavy teaching demands of the Sorbonne. He opted instead to accept a post at the University of Montpellier, located in the south of France on the Mediterranean coast, with his partner Anne, a noted Proust scholar, whom he married in 1958. There he was able to balance the lighter teaching demands with an ambitious writing schedule and extensive travel. He remained at the University of Montpellier until his retirement in 1982.

Between the publication of *The Essence of Manifestation* (1963) and *Material Phenomenology* (1990), Henry published a number of interesting and controversial books on topics such as politics, economics, art, and psychoanalysis, in addition to writing several novels. Insofar as a discussion of those works remains beyond the scope of this introduction, our sole focus here will be to trace the connection between *The Essence of Manifestation* and *Material Phenomenology*. As noted, *The Essence of Manifestation* sought to show that the history of Western thought, in spite of its apparent differences, shares an underlying commitment to ontological monism, which is to say, it understands the appearing of all being in terms of transcendence. Setting himself against this tradition, Henry argues that there exists a more fundamental mode of being, immanence, which is the origin of all transcendence whatsoever. Immanence is a mode of being that is completely free from all the traits of transcendence, which is to say that it is without intentionality, without representation, without horizon, and without exteriority. This radical immanence does not reveal itself in the light of the world but rather though auto-affectivity, as a feeling of oneself in the suffering and enjoyment of one's own life. The auto-affectivity of life, in its radical immanence, is what makes all knowledge and activity possible, including the phenomenological knowledge that seeks to provide a "presuppositionless" basis for all thought. As Henry notes, the radical immanence of life makes phenomenology possible as a phenomenology of "absolute subjectivity as well as the essential questions bound to it, viz. the development of a phenomenology and a phenomenological philosophy of lived experience, the ego, self-knowledge, inner life and its proper temporality, the general structure of experience and its essential forms."[5] While this statement establishes the radical immanence of life as the necessary starting point for Husserlian phenomenology, the claim is not elaborated in much detail in *The Essence of Manifestation*, where the engagement with Heidegger is the primary point of emphasis.

No major shift in Henry's thought takes place after *The Essence of Manifestation*, but *Material Phenomenology* is of great interest and importance because it provides the detailed elaboration of why and how Husserlian phenomenology must be rooted in the radical immanence of life, which was lacking in the earlier work. In fact, the title of this work originates from a question posed by Didier Franck in conjunction with a 1987 issue of the journal *Philosophie* devoted to Henry's thought. While preparing that issue, Franck sent a list of questions to Henry, one of which specifically asked Henry to clarify the relation between his own "material phenomenology" and Husserl's "hyletic phenomenology." Taking up that question, Henry returned to Husserl in order to clarify his understanding of material phenomenology and its specific task; his answer to that question comprises the first chapter of this book.

The first chapter of *Material Phenomenology* offers a patient and detailed analysis of Husserl's treatment of the notion of *hyle* (matter) in some key passages in *Ideas I* (1913) and in his *Lectures on the Internal Consciousness of Time* (1905). While part of Husserl's novelty consists in the discovery that all consciousness is impressional, Henry shows that a general devaluation of *hyle* and hyletic phenomenology nevertheless occurs in those analyses. *Hyle*, which refers to the non-intentional stuff entering into conscious experience, is understood solely as matter existing for the sake of form, that is, for the ek-stasis of intentionality. While this impressional element is the necessary basis for intentionality, Husserl abandons the impressional element as such—the *Ur-impression*—that is the essence of phenomenality, in order to focus on the eidetic analysis of intentionality. In contrast, the task of material phenomenology, on Henry's view, is precisely to recover the significance of the impressional element of consciousness. Material phenomenology finds its significance to be rooted in the life that gives birth and growth to consciousness.

The second chapter examines Husserl's reflections on the phenomenological method in *The Idea of Phenomenology* (1907) and engages the important methodological reflections in §7 of Heidegger's *Being and Time* (1927). Through his examination of the development of the phenomenological reduction in Husserl's thought, Henry shows that the reduction is ultimately a reduction to transcendence. The phenomenological reduction enables every experience to be made into an object of pure seeing. While this method enables consciousness to turn toward the performances of conscious life as objects of reflection, Henry shows that, at the same time, this signifies a turning away from the actual, lived *cogitatio*. So, even though the *cogitatio* is the prior condition for phenomenological reflection, it is lost to phenomenological reflection when it is converted into a given, as an object of consciousness, in phenomenological reflection. The methodological task of material phenomenology, then, is to replace the reduction to transcendence that opens onto the intentional life of the subject with a reduction to immanence that opens onto a subject who is held in the embrace of the pathos of life.

The third chapter examines Husserl's treatment of the intersubjective community in his fifth Cartesian meditation (1931), and in so doing, constitutes a tacit reply to the common charge that Henry's account of the radical immanence of life ultimately leads to solipsism. While Husserl's account of the intersubjective community is an attempt to overcome solipsism as well, it begins from the solitary ego by reducing the ego to its sphere of ownness. However, as Henry shows, Husserl quickly demotes the sphere of ownness to the level of the psycho-physical ego. The ego's perception of its own body then becomes the basis for pairing its own body with the perception of the other's body, and thus by analogy, for overlaying the other's body with an unperceived conscious life that is analogous to the ego's own conscious life. There are many problems with Husserl's account of intersubjectivity, but for Henry all of these problems can ultimately be traced back to Husserl's decision to promote transcendence over the immanence of life. The alter ego is not perceived, according to Henry, precisely because the ego's sphere of ownness, defined by the auto-affectivity of life, is itself unperceived. The intersubjective community, therefore, is joined together not through a shared perception of the world—or transcendence—but through the pathos of life. The notion of life, Henry suggests, can thus explain both the individuality of the individual and the individual's participation in a shared, affective community of the living.

Having provided this brief overview of *Material Phenomenology*, I would like to offer a few suggestions as to how this text might be engaged productively. Although the three chapters of this book were composed as independent essays, each offers a careful analysis of an influential Husserlian text. Since these essays are so closely aligned with the Husserlian texts, the reader can gain the most from this text by first reading Husserl's original texts on his or her own and then rereading them along with Henry here. In so doing, the reader can appreciate the craft of Henry's careful readings and possibly even detect distortions in them. The more advanced reader might also want to explore differences between the French and English translations of Husserl's texts, a matter that becomes particularly acute with respect to the concept of life. The semantic reservoir of the concept of life is richer in German, where there is an evident connection between *Leben* and *Erlebnisse*, as well as in French, where there likewise exists a connection between *la vie* and *le vécu*. This linguistic connection disappears in English, however, where the term *Erlebnis* is commonly translated as a "mental process." This is only one example, among others, in which the advanced reader may profit from consulting the original German texts (with which Henry was very familiar) for a deeper evaluation of Henry's argument.

Another fruitful connection for readers to explore has to do with a contemporaneous work in French phenomenology, Jean-Luc Marion's *Reduction and Givenness* (1989). In the preface, Marion acknowledges how much Michel Henry's "faithful friendship and his example of philosophical probity have sustained me."[6] While these two thinkers are commonly joined together as part of the "theological turn" in French philosophy, these two works in particular are worthy of comparison insofar as they present their respective authors' visions of phenomenology. To compare the two works, one might begin from a 1991 essay, "Quatre principes de la phénoménologie," in which Henry addresses Marion's work directly.[7] There Henry credits Marion with the development of a new phenomenological principle: "all the more reduction, all the more givenness." Henry finds this principle to be amenable to his own thought, insofar as it understands the task of phenomenology to be a matter of opening a domain of pure phenomenological givenness. Yet, he argues, Marion fails to appreciate the pure givenness opened up by his radical reduction of objects and the world. Marion's account of pure givenness in terms of the pure form of the call, according to Henry, remains indistinguishable from the appearing of the call of being in Heidegger, because it separates the sender of the call from the receiver. It thus remains modeled on the ecstatic mode of appearing, which is characteristic of the entire history of Western thought. What Marion fails to appreciate, according to Henry, is that if pure appearing can be described as a pure call, this call must be that of Life. The pure call is thus one in which the sender and receiver are no longer separated by any distance whatever; instead, they are joined in the immediacy of life. Life's immediate givenness of itself to itself in auto-affection is thus the centerpiece of Henry's material phenomenology.

Finally, material phenomenology points to an entirely new set of tasks for phenomenology to carry out, including the clarification of what makes appearing into an appearance and the description of the phenomenological matter out of which it is made. The phenomenological matter of appearing, as Henry suggests, is the pathetic flesh of our life. Yet, the phenomenological analyses of the flesh and life remain undeveloped here, as do their applications to relevant aspects of concrete life. While the phenomenological analysis of the flesh is taken up in part by Henry's overtly theological work *Incarnation: Une philosophie de la chair* (*Incarnation: A Philosophy of the Flesh*), for the most part these tasks still remain incomplete.[8] My hope is that the English translation of this work will provide an impetus for others to take up these important tasks in future investigations of their own.

A few final comments on details of the translation are in order here. All italics in the text are taken from Henry's original text. In order to highlight Henry's own points of emphasis, I did not carry over the italics from the English translation of Husserl's texts. All citations of Husserl refer to both the German original and the English translation. I have slightly modified the English translation in a few cases where it helped to maintain the flow of Henry's point. All such modifications are indicated in the text and are necessitated by slight differences between the French and English translations of Husserl.

Three terminological issues need to be highlighted. First, in speaking of the passive dimension of auto-affectivity, Henry often uses the term *pathétique*, which has been translated here simply as "pathetic." In spite of the negative connotations that this term may have in ordinary English, the reader should keep in mind its etymological link to the Greek *pathos*, meaning feeling or passion. So, in speaking, for example, of the pathetic flesh of life, Henry is placing an emphasis on the passive and affective dimension of the flesh. Second, in speaking about the members of the affective community, Henry employs the term *vivants*. Where possible, I have rendered this as "the living" but in some cases have been compelled to opt for "living beings." With respect to the latter term, one should bear in mind that Henry seeks to distinguish "the living" from "beings" in the sense of external objects, and so the emphasis should remain on the fact that "living beings" are alive and not that they are beings. Third, as noted, there is a semantic slippage that occurs in passing from the German *Erlebnis* to the English "mental process" that does not occur in the French equivalent, *vécu*. One option here would be to translate this term as "lived experience," as many English translators of the French *vécu* have done. Since Henry's work is an engagement with Husserl's texts, I chose to follow the accepted English translation of Husserl's *Erlebnisse* as "mental processes" but have also indicated Henry's use of the term *vécu* in parentheses wherever it occurs. This decision should be satisfactory as long as the reader is aware that for Husserl the term "mental process" does not refer narrowly to a process of reasoning but broadly to all the various activities of conscious life, such as knowing, willing, desiring, feeling, and so forth. The only significant loss here involves the etymological connection to life, but if Henry's argument is philosophically sound, it should be able to stand without this explicit connection.

List of Abbreviations

Edmund Husserl

Hua I   *Husserliana 1. Cartesianische Meditationen und Pariser Vorträge*, ed. Stephen Strasser (The Hague: Martinus Nijhoff, 1950); *Cartesian Meditations: An Introduction to Phenomenology*, trans. Dorion Cairns (The Hague: Martinus Nijhoff, 1960).

Hua II   *Husserliana 2. Die Idee der Phänomenologie. Fünf Vorlesungen*, ed. Walter Biemel (The Hague: Martinus Nijhoff, 1950); *The Idea of Phenomenology*, trans. Lee Hardy (Dordrecht: Kluwer Academic, 1999).

Hua III *Husserliana 3. Ideen zu einer reinen Phänomenologie und phänomenologischen Philosophie. Erstes Buch. Allgemeine Einführung in die reine Phänomenologie*, ed. Karl Schuhmann (The Hague: Martinus Nijhoff, 1976); *Ideas Pertaining to a Pure Phenomenology and to a Phenomenological Philosophy: First Book—General Introduction to a Pure Phenomenology*, trans. Fred Kersten (The Hague: Martinus Nijhoff, 1982).

Hua IV   *Husserliana 4. Ideen zu einer reinen Phänomenologie und phänomenologischen Philosophie. Zweites Buch. Phänomenologische Untersuchungen zur Konstitution*, ed. Marly Biemel (The Hague: Martinus Nijhoff, 1952); *Ideas Pertaining to a Pure Phenomenology and to a Phenomenological Philosophy: Second Book—Studies in the Phenomenology of Constitution*, trans. Richard Rojcewicz and André Schuwer (Dordrecht: Kluwer Academic, 1989).

Hua X   *Husserliana 10. Zur Phänomenologie des inneren Zeitbewusstseins (1893–1917)*, ed. Rudolf Boehm (The Hague: Martinus Nijhoff, 1966); *On the Phenomenology of the Consciousness of Internal Time (1893–1917)*, trans. John Barnett Brough (Dordrecht: Kluwer Academic, 1991).

Martin Heidegger

SZ   *Sein und Zeit* (Tübingen: Max Niemeyer, 1927); *Being and Time*, trans. Joan Stambaugh (Albany: State University of New York Press, 1996).

Introduction: The Question of Phenomenology

With the collapse of the Parisian fashions of the last decades, and most notably structuralism, which represented its most widespread form because it was the most superficial, and with the return of the human sciences (which sought to replace philosophy but only offered an external viewpoint on the human being) to their proper place, phenomenology increasingly seems to be the principal movement of the thought of our times. The "return of Husserl" is the return of a capacity for intelligibility, which is due to the invention of a method and, first of all, a question in which the essence of philosophy can be rediscovered. Phenomenology will be to the twentieth century what German idealism was to the nineteenth, what empiricism was to the eighteenth, what Descartes was to the seventeenth, what Thomas Aquinas and Duns Scotus were to scholasticism, what Plato and Aristotle were to antiquity. In order to take its place now in this prestigious gallery among the highest figures of thought, must not phenomenology itself, like those grand models, belong to the past?

That would be so only if the presuppositions that together make up the question of phenomenology had exhausted their resources and had unfolded all their implications. In the opinion of many, this would seem to be the case. What does a thinker such as Merleau-Ponty, in spite of his great talent, contribute that is truly new in relation to Husserl, Heidegger, or Scheler? And since then, has the phenomenological movement been able to allow for any breakthroughs whose premises would not have been discernable in its founders?

Today the renewal of phenomenology is only possible on one condition: that the question that determines it entirely and that is philosophy's own raison d'être be renewed. This does not mean that it should be expanded, corrected, amended, or still less abandoned for the sake of another question, but that it should be radicalized in such a way that what depends on it would be overturned and, subsequently, everything would in fact be changed.

The question of phenomenology, which alone confers a proper object to philosophy, is what makes it into an autonomous discipline—the fundamental discipline of knowledge—and not just a mere reflection after the fact on what the other sciences have found. This question is no longer concerned with the phenomena but the mode of their givenness, their phenomenality, not with what appears but with appearing. The invaluable contribution of historical phenomenology is to become aware of this appearing and to analyze it in and of itself. This is its theme. Again, this must not simply be the repetition of the traditional philosophical problem of consciousness or the Greek *aletheia*. For the illusion of common sense, science, and past philosophies is to understand the being of the phenomenon always as a first putting at a distance, the arrival of an Outside in which everything becomes visible, a "phenomenon," in the light of this Outside. It is being-beyond-beings. Through its difference with beings, the ek-stasis creates phenomenality in whatever manner it is represented, be it implicit or explicit, naive or philosophical.

To radicalize the question of phenomenology is not only to aim for a pure phenomenality but also to seek out the mode according to which it originally becomes a phenomenon—the substance, the stuff, the phenomenological matter of which it is made, its phenomenologically pure materiality. That is the task of material phenomenology. Prior to the being-toward-the-outside in which everything is properly speaking placed outside of itself and in which every reality is *a priori* emptied and dispossessed of itself and thus becomes its contrary, an irreality, and prior to the abandonment and undoing that is called death and that would be unable to exist on its own, material phenomenology is devoted to the discovery of the reign of a phenomenality that is constructed in such a surprising way that the thought that always thinks about the world never thinks about it. To the internal structure of this originary manifestation, there belongs no Outside, no Separation, no Ek-stasis. Its phenomenological substance is not visibility. None of the categories that have been used by philosophy, since the Greeks at any rate, are appropriate for it.

Material phenomenology is able to designate this invisible phenomenological substance. It is not a nothing but rather an affect, or put otherwise, it is what makes every affect, ultimately every affection, and thus every thing possible. The phenomenological substance that material phenomenology has in view is the pathetic immediacy in which life experiences itself. Life is itself nothing other than this pathetic embrace and, in this way, is phenomenality itself according to the how of its original phenomenalization.

Life is thus not a something, like the object of biology, but the principle of every thing. It is a phenomenological life in the radical sense where life defines the essence of pure phenomenality and accordingly of being insofar as being is coextensive with the phenomenon and founded on it. For what could I know about a being that could not appear? Because life is the original phenomenalization at the core of being and thus what makes it be, one must reverse the traditional hierarchy that subordinates life to being under the pretext that it would be necessary for life itself "to be." As such, the living would delineate only a region of being, a regional ontology. But the being to which life is submitted is Greek being, the being of a worldly being, which would be thought and conceived starting on the basis of the world. Such a being would still only be a dead being or rather a nonbeing, if the ek-stasis in which its proper phenomenality unfolds were not auto-affected in the immediacy of the pathos of Life. So Life always founds what we call "being" rather than the contrary.[1]

The studies collected in this book are all organized around the question of phenomenology, and each one of them poses this question in its own way. The first shows, with respect to the problem of time, how material phenomenology can be distinguished from classical phenomenology. The question of phenomenology is exposed here under a harsh light. For the interrogation of time is Husserl's way to think how consciousness, which is to say phenomenality, manifests itself. From the outset, phenomenology is unable to provide a true response to its own question because that response is sought from intentionality, and the self-revelation of absolute subjectivity is understood from the outset as a self-constitution. In phenomenology, the ultimate constituent is deprived of every assignable phenomenological status and is delivered over to the "anonymous." Phenomenology's hermeneutical deviation, which marks its historical destiny and finds its result in the ontological pessimism of the current epoch (whose fashions referred to above are only its latest, quite ridiculous expression), is contained entirely in this aborted beginning.

If life, as something essentially foreign to ek-stasis, conceals itself in principle from every conceivable visualization, then how can one display it in any theory whatsoever or in any view, however that term might be construed? Is not a phenomenology of the invisible a contradiction in terms? In the arrival itself of life as its pathetic auto-affection and thus as radically immanent, a Self is born whose phenomenological materiality is this pathos. Is not this "Self," supported by an acosmic subjectivity but also enclosed by it, given over to solipsism? The two objections raised against the theses of *The Essence of Manifestation* since its publication and often repeated since then concern, first, the very possibility of constructing a theory of pure affectivity, and second, the possibility of a pathetic and acosmic ipseity ever entering into relation with an other of the same kind and engaging in an actual and concrete intersubjective relation with the other.

The second study, which is devoted to the phenomenological method, shows that classical phenomenology runs up against the impossibility of providing a theoretical knowledge of absolute subjectivity and so itself offers the proof that transcendental life withdraws from every intentional approach, from evidence, and the "pure seeing" of the phenomenological reduction. The extraordinary path unconsciously followed by Husserl to try to overcome this aporia is the striking proof of the non-ek-static status of life. This would be a phenomenological status, however, if it is true that the eidetic method, which is a method of substitution, is constantly supported by the profusion of the original givenness that it fails to recognize.

The third study joins together two texts related to the problem referred to as that of the "experience of the other." The first establishes the failure of intentionality on the very terrain on which it was supposed to prevail. Does not the opening to the alterity of a "world" found every relation to others? Does not *In-der-Welt-Sein* found every conceivable *Mit-Sein*? The failure of these self-evident theses is loaded with consequences. In fact, it shows that only the renunciation of what Western thought counts as evidence, which is ultimately the evidence of perception, can clear the path that leads back to the Essential. Paradoxically, while life in itself does not refer to anything other than itself, it provides the milieu in which all intersubjectivity whatsoever can take place. And the paradox may be less than it might seem to be, if it is in the experience of a radically immanent subject that life arrives to itself and seizes its own being. That by which a Self becomes a Self, the way in which it expands and grows on its own, is also the way in which everything that can affect it originally arrives, including the "being" of the other. The ego and the alter ego have a common birth, a shared essence. Through this, they "communicate" as living beings. Would it be a surprise, then, if life were a transcendental affectivity that all intersubjectivity, by drawing its essence from life, would inevitably take on the form of a pathetic community?

Allow me to say a word about the sources of these three studies. The first was written in response to a question from the editors of the journal *Philosophie* for the 1987 summer edition, which was devoted to my work. They asked: "How does material phenomenology, which your project is called, differ from what Husserl calls hyletic phenomenology?" The second essay was planned for a long time and is published here for the first time. It establishes the possibility of the "knowledge" of invisible subjectivity. The first text of the third study is from a lecture given at the École Normale Supérieure in Paris on April 23, 1988, in Jean-François Courtine's seminar and repeated at the Katholieke Universiteit Leuven for a colloquium marking the fiftieth year after Husserl's death. It was published in the proceedings of that colloquium. The second was the topic of a forum at the Collège Internationale de Philosophie on December 7, 1987, in the context of its annual program on research devoted to the question of community. The idea of linking these various analyses in the present order was put forward in six seminars given in March 1989 at the University of Washington with Mikkel Borch-Jacobsen.

A final word on the method used in these investigations. One will not fail to be surprised by the small number and brevity of the texts that support this meditation. This is not a work on Husserl, much less a "dialogue" with him. It is a matter of reflecting on the decisions that were made at the outset and on the presuppositions to which he never returns again to assess, along with the dynamism of the doctrine at its initial state, its essential lacuna, in short, the absence of a phenomenology of transcendental life on which, however, the entire edifice depends for its foundation. In this regard, the lectures of 1905 and 1907 are the most significant.

The consideration of other texts could have led to the same conclusions. For example, take the dissolution of absolute subjectivity in a "Heraclitean flux," so misunderstood by Husserl and so unacceptable to him. In truth, its explosion, its destruction, its dispersion would occur once one replaces its Archi-revelation, unperceived in itself, with the appearance of "lived experiences" in the first ek-stasis of time. This is affirmed by Husserl in nearly identical terms in every period of his thought: in *Cartesian Meditations* (§ 20), in the "difficulties" of the *Crisis* (§ 52), and in the 1907 lectures, which are analyzed here. As far as the unpublished manuscripts, these are mere working notes with an often programmatic character that cannot be opposed to the published and signed work. A systematic reading of them, which has yet to be done, would certainly show that it is the problem of the Archi-givenness, thought temporally as the givenness of the "living present," that they stumble up against repeatedly. Perhaps only a material phenomenology can discover the transcendental clue for this obscure side of the work, which remains pending, while its other side is illuminated by intentionality.

Things differ entirely depending on whether they are immersed in the pathos of life in which they never see themselves, or whether they are held in front of a regard. These are not, it seems, the same thing. To the former category would belong drives, forces, affects—everything that we are deep down within ourselves, everything that matters. They do not belong in immanence simply because they are put there by chance but because they are only possible there. The same, however, goes for the regard, for seeing, which never sees itself, and consequently for knowledge and science itself. Everything falls back into life and only has its being in it; everything is alive.

The task of material phenomenology is immense. It is not simply to be attached to another order of phenomena that remained neglected up to now but to rethink everything, if one can think reality. Every sphere of reality must become the object of a new analysis that goes back to its invisible dimension. And this concerns material nature as well, which is a living cosmos.

Since material phenomenology implies the revival of philosophical questioning in its entirety, it offers a future to phenomenology and to philosophy itself. At the same time, it discovers a new past. The philosophy that reflects on itself and becomes its own history can no longer understand itself in light of the presuppositions that have guided it since its inception, in such a way that this history of philosophy would change nothing about its history and would only constitute its last phase. Without a doubt, here one must listen to Jean-Luc Marion's proposal "to locate, to exhume, and to think another history of philosophy, irreducible to the 'history of metaphysics' elaborated by Heidegger."[2]

This immense task is at once the task of understanding reality and the self-understanding of this understanding. This task has been carried out in part elsewhere, specifically, with respect to the problems of the manifestation of the body, economic reality, the "unconscious," and aesthetic life in its antithetical relation to the universe of modernity. But this task is not the purpose of these short studies. Here it is only a matter of giving an idea as to what material phenomenology is, the method that makes it possible as a phenomenology of the invisible, and of testing its capacity for innovation in a domain as difficult and as seemingly irreducible to its premises as that of intersubjectivity. A systematic study of intersubjectivity will be the topic of a subsequent work.[3]

1

Hyletic Phenomenology and Material Phenomenology

In §85 of *Ideas I*, Husserl offers an explicit definition of what he means by "hyletic phenomenology."[1] This definition puts into play the key findings of phenomenology, and in some way, the basis of its essential theses. In the flow of absolute subjectivity or consciousness, the real and irreal moments are distinguished. The irreal moments belong to the noema. When I perceive a tree, the tree is not really contained in the consciousness perceiving it. The tree does not belong to its substance in any way. It stands before consciousness or outside of consciousness. And if subjectivity is reality, then consequently the tree is outside of reality and in an irreality. Within subjectivity itself, however, the material or hyletic moments must be distinguished from intentional moments. The latter animate the former and give them a sense. In the perception of the tree, for example, there are sense contents, such as color data, that serve as the basis for this perception. Through them, the conscious regard is directed toward the tree as a real object, which is to say as an object transcending consciousness. Husserl was able to distinguish rigorously between contents, on one hand, understood as objective "sense qualities" that are properties of the thing and thus are its noematic characteristics and, on the other hand, the purely sensuous lived experiences that are the subjective impressions (visual, sonorous, and so on) through which the objective moments of the object are "adumbrated." The essence of these primary sensuous impressions—which are subjective adumbrations in which the world presents itself—is precisely that they are inherent to subjectivity as its real elements, just like the intentionality that constitutes the object on the basis of them. What distinguishes the sensuous impressions from intentionality is that they do not carry within them the structure of intentionality, being never in nor through themselves intentional. Husserl writes, "The sensuous element, which has in itself nothing pertaining to intentionality" (Hua III 172/203). The essence of the *hyle* is thus determined in two respects: positively, through its belonging to the reality of absolute subjectivity as constitutive of its stuff and its own being; and negatively, by the exclusion of every intentionality from it.

The twofold definition of the sensuous *hyle* in both positive and negative terms puts some deep questions before us. If the essence of *hyle* excludes intentionality from itself, how can the essence of *hyle* nonetheless unite with intentionality at the heart of absolute subjectivity? Moreover, how can it define the real moment of absolute subjectivity and enter into it as a real constituent, if the intentional *morphe* is invested with the same power and status?[2] Can the reality of subjectivity reside at once in an essence that fulfills the transcendence of being as an object and in an essence from which this transcendence is absent? In this context, the title of §97, "The hyletic and noetic moments as really inherent moments of mental processes (*le vécu*)," appears to us as an enigma.[3] This point is taken up again unequivocally in the development of the argument when Husserl states that "not only the hyletic moments (the sensed colors, sounds, etc.), but also the animating construals—thus both together: the appearing of the color, the sound, and thus of any quality whatever of the object—belong to the "really inherent" composition of the mental process (*le vécu*)" (Hua III 203–204/238).

If two essences differ absolutely, together they cannot promote the homogeneity from which every reality draws its possibility. Instead, this implies that there exists a foundational link between them such that one of them underlies the other one and, in spite of their difference, serves as its basis. The essential question is which one of these, the non-intentional *hyle* or the intentional *morphe*, is subjectivity, and thus which one of these disciplines, hyletic phenomenology or the phenomenology of intentional consciousness, is supreme. That is also a question about essences in the sense that it can only be solved through eidetic analysis. Through variations of the components of the real, it must be shown which of these can disappear without this reality itself disappearing and which of these cannot be varied or eliminated because it constitutes the reality or "essence" of subjectivity. With respect to the reality of absolute subjectivity, one must imagine it, in turn, without its material component and without its intentional component in order to see what, if anything, subsists each time as the phenomenological residue.

Whatever does subsist is certainly a foundation. It needs nothing other than itself in order to exist because everything else has been removed and it still "exists." It is also a foundation for everything else, because if anything else is there, then it must be there as well. As an initial remark, let me put it this way. Material phenomenology, as I conceive it, results from a radical reduction of every transcendence that yields the hyletic or impressional component as the underlying essence of subjectivity. However fantastic and inconceivable this reduction may seem, it has nonetheless been produced in the history of human thought, for example, with Descartes's *cogito*. Doubt can only call into question the world and every possible world, to the extent that it first has already let go of *the relation to the world as such*, that is, intentionality. Naturally, the radical reduction of every transcendence can only become possible and have a sense to the extent that it can show, at the end of its proceedings, what subsists when transcendence is no longer there. Descartes did not push his analysis further. His understanding of the foundation is shrouded in an ambiguity fraught with consequences, referring at the same time to evidence and to that which, resting underneath and supporting it, is insurmountably excluded from evidence. This ambiguity shows that the task of material phenomenology remains to be carried out. Before sketching out this task, let us return to the Husserlian text.

Husserl is not unaware of the crucial questions we have raised. Far from it, he perceives them in the dazzling clarity of the eidetic regard. In the flow of lived experience, this regard asks "whether everywhere and necessarily such sensuous mental processes (*le vécu*) bear some animating construing or other (with all the characteristics which this, in turn, demands and makes possible), whether, as we also say, they always have intentive functions, is not to be decided here. On the other hand, we must likewise leave it undecided at first if the characteristics essentially making up intentionality can have concreteness without having sensuous foundations" (Hua III 172/204). It is evident that these questions about essences are thrown straightaway into the eidetic analysis in which one must determine if *A* is possible without *B* or if *B* is possible without *A*, since these two possibilities are also labeled "matter without form and form without matter" (Hua III 173/204; translation modified).

However, the text does not respond to these enormous questions whose resolution would require the use of an infallible method and which were created for this method. The text cited above concludes as follows: "it is not to be decided here . . . we likewise leave it undecided" in order to finish with an "at first" which means "whatever the case may be." What a strange indecisiveness when what comes under investigation is no less than the internal structure of the Archi-foundation. One might say that the questioning is simply deferred. In fact, it will never be taken up again under this thematic form. The few statements pertaining to the original cleavage of *hyle* and *morphe* will only evade or disguise this essential discovery. Why this silence or powerlessness?

The passage that follows helps us to understand this. What can be recognized there is an unperceived slippage that the analysis does not address. At the end of this slippage, the initial concept of matter is modified to the point that its original sense is substituted with another one, thus taking hyletic phenomenology outside of its proper domain and into that of intentional and constitutive phenomenology. "Matter" initially refers to the essence of the impression, or of what is originally tantamount to it, sensation. Matter is in fact the matter out of which the impression is made: its stuff, its substance as a manner of speaking, the impressional, or the sensuous as such. To speak of "sense data" or "hyletic moments of mental processes (*le vécu*)" is to say nothing more than that. It is to be confined to the "sensuous color" (*Empfindungsfarbe*), to the pure sonorous impression reduced to itself, to what is in itself (the reduction is indeed the return to the things themselves) and, in a similar way, to pure pain, to pure joy, and to all of the lived experiences (*le vécu*) defined and demarcated by their impressional character. Once again, they are nothing more than that and, as belonging to the *hyle*, they are non-intentional.

Very soon in the analysis, however, perhaps even really from the outset, there emerges the reality from which phenomenological analysis borrows its structure and from which it is never completely able to free its thinking. "Matter" is overdetermined by the role that it plays within the totality of the noetic processes in which it is included. This role turns it into a matter for the intentional acts that take hold of it and that, starting from the content it provides each time, constitute the object. Thus, the sense data, the hyletic "colors," and the sonorous impressions take on the role of "adumbrations" through which the sense qualities or the noematic moments of the object are grasped intentionally. Husserl claims: "Sensuous data are given as matter for intentional complexes or sense-bestowals, belonging to different levels" (Hua III 172/204; translation modified). *Matter is not the matter of the impression, the impressional or impressionality as such; instead, it is the matter of the act that informs it, a matter for this form. The givenness of this matter does not belong to it, either. It is not matter itself that is given or matter that gives itself, in virtue of what it is, through its own impressional character.* It gives itself to form, that is, it is given by form. It gives itself to form in order to be informed, constituted, and apprehended by it. But to constitute, even if we disregard all transcendent construals, means to let something be seen, to let something come into being as a phenomenon, and this means to give it. "Sensible givens, sensuous data" must be understood in the sense whereby "being given as matter for intentional complexes" is being given in a certain way, as something traversed by an intentional regard that casts it before itself and gives it to be seen. The "sensible appearances" through which the world is given to us do not give themselves. They are only appearances or phenomena inasmuch as they are animated by a noetic intention and come to appear through it.

We said earlier that Husserl left the fundamental problem of the conscious unity of the hyletic and intentional components of lived experience unresolved. He was unable to show how this unity resides in the reality of absolute subjectivity, and moreover, unable to define this reality. Here we see at least how he interprets it; how and why it is not a problem for him. These components are related to one another as what brings something into the condition of being a phenomenon and what is brought into phenomenality. In the "reality" of mental processes (*le vécu*), the relation between sensuous and intentional moments, between matter and form, is a unitary relation established between appearing and what appears in it. It is their ontico-ontological embrace. Husserl states that "not only the hyletic moments (colors, sensuous sounds) but also the construals that animate it—thus both together: the appearing of the color, the sound and thus of any quality whatever of the object—belong to the "really inherent" composition of the mental processes" (Hua III 203–204/238).

But if *hyle* is united with *morphe*, as what appears is united with its appearing, then *hyle* becomes originally and in itself lacking of the latter, that is, of the capacity to carry out the work of manifestation in and by itself. In and by itself, it is nothing more than a blind content, and that is the reason why it is "given as matter for intentional complexes." By "animating" it, the intentional complexes can cast light on *hyle* and turn it into a "phenomenon." In the unity that is supposed to be explained in this way, it is not merely the case that difference reigns and finds its field of play there; more profoundly, a radical dissymmetry is introduced between the two components of absolute subjectivity: the hyletic and the intentional. The hyletic is charged with giving its content, the impression, to experience, while the intentional proposes it as a content of experience in the light that it produces. Might the real unity, which is to say the actual unity, of *hyle* and *morphe* also signify *hyle*'s real inherence—as a real constituent—in the reality of subjectivity, if *hyle* determines appearing and defines it? It is, if not the unity of *hyle* and *morphe*, at least the internal unity of subjectivity itself that comes into question now. This concerns the possibility of appearing really to include in itself, in its pure phenomenality, that which remains radically foreign to it. Is it not necessary, instead, that this opaque element should already be held at a distance, in the first Outside of visibility, which is the work of intentionality and is actually "constituted" by it? For this reason, Husserl can and must write: "*Intentionality . . . is also like a universal medium which ultimately bears in itself all mental processes (le vécu), even those which are not characterized as intentive*" (Hua III 171/203). This is the case inasmuch as mental processes, even impressional ones, are always already ejected outside of themselves in this site of visibility, which pertains to transcendence, which is a first world.

This ejection into the ontological transcendence of *morphe* signifies a dejection of *hyle*'s own being into the ontic, as the passages from *Ideas I* to which our reflection has been limited up to now already attest. The examination of hyletic data is presented there with a striking lack of rigor. This is because for a thought that supposedly obeys the *telos* of eidetic analysis—and does so for ultimate reasons that will be analyzed in the next chapter—it does not proceed in this way but in the mere amalgam of a pre-philosophical enumeration. This is not simply due to a terminological difficulty, to which the major portion of the discussion is devoted and from which no true clarification results. Instead, the difficulty results from an essential question that is continually avoided. The impressional mental processes (*le vécu*), the former "primary contents" of the *Logical Investigations*, comprise the sensory contents through which the transcendent objects of perception are adumbrated. In some respect, they form the phenomenological residue of what is found in perception when its transcendence is bracketed. If one calls this impressional *quid*, this pure sensuousness, "sensibility," one finds it again among the group of mental processes (*vécus*) from the affective and volitional sphere and among the drives that play such a large role in human life. One might believe then that the first putting at a distance of sense data, which makes it so difficult to distinguish them from the noematic moments of the thing on which they are immediately projected, owes to the fact that the sense data are considered here in terms of perception, when the apprehending regard traverses them. By contrast, in the case of affective and desiring mental processes (*vécus*), their radical immanence is their impressional being as such, which excludes every transcendence. This radical immanence should have been recognized more easily.

Just the opposite occurs with Husserl. Once the extension of the impressional character to different types of mental processes leads "affective states [*Gefühle*] and sensuous impulses" to be included in sensibility, it thus leads to the extension of "the originally narrow term sensuousness to the spheres of emotion and will, namely to the intentive mental process in which sensuous Data belonging to the designated spheres make their appearance as functioning 'stuffs'" (Hua III 173/205). Thus, it appears that these affective and desiring mental processes are themselves intentional and that their impressional and affective element does not constitute their essence. This means that they are affective and desiring mental processes, but first of all, they are simply mental processes. What originally gives and reveals them—the impressional and the affective—are only "sense data" that "present themselves as 'matter,'" *just like the sense data of perception*, in order to provide a content for the intentional act that will cast them outside of themselves and into the truth of the object. Once again, matter is not the matter of the impression and its stuff, nor the impressionality of the impression, nor the affectivity of the affective. Instead, it is the matter of an act. Its role is to provide the content for this act so that, by starting from this content, it can fulfill its own proper role. In and through the passage of intentionality, its role is that of showing and of opening the space of light where this content and every thing will give itself to be seen and will become a "given."

What would the manifestation of this purely impressional element be, apart from the role in which it gives itself to intentionality and serves as the matter for intentionality? Does the impressionality of the impression, its affectivity, already carry out, in and of itself, a function in manifestation, a phenomenological function? If we were to consider only the pages on which we are now working, we would be left completely uncertain. It is the phenomenologist who reflects on sense data and, in a privileged way, on the role they play as matter in perception. Then it would be in this reflection and in a specific type of intentionality that the phenomenologist would seize upon them, with an evidence that does not belong originally to the impressional element itself. For example, Husserl writes: "Let us reflect on sensation, on adumbrations: we seize upon them as evident givens" (Hua III 203/237). Or it is the case that we want to know what they are before they are grasped reflectively and thus we do not know them, as, for example, when Husserl writes, "in the former [the perceptual mental process], they were contained as really inherent moments, but they were not perceived therein, not seized upon as objects" (Hua III 205/240). What, then, were they? This question about the original revelation of absolute subjectivity is the crux of Husserlian phenomenology. The difficulty is handled by recourse to the theme of the noema; the analysis of the noema enables the nature of the noeses that constitute it to be defined. Husserl asserts: "We can designate all those noetic components only by appealing to the noematic Object and its moments" (Hua III 204/238). *But what would be the basis for this designation when there is no longer a noema, which is to say precisely, for hyle,* which is clearly one of the two noetic components?

One might say that they are the noematic moments of the perceived object. It is the green of the tree that calls for me to think this purely subjective sensation of color on the basis of which it is constituted. But when "sensuous appearing" in the sense of a transcendent presentation of the object's noematic quality is proposed as a text that must be deciphered in order to determine what impression corresponds to it in pure subjectivity, nothing is actually known about the original revelation of this impression, that is, of its subjectivity. It is not by chance that the impressional data are revealed on the basis of the phenomenon of perception and its mediation and that they are referred to as "adumbrations," more precisely, as the adumbrations of things. For the phenomenological tradition, this is a way of bypassing an obstacle that unfortunately cannot be bypassed. The case of perception is one in which a noematic correlate corresponds to the impression. But what is the case, one wonders, when no correlate of this kind can be produced? This is what happens with feelings and with the entire group of mental processes from the affective domain, including desires and volitions. It is impossible to define a fear, an anxiety, a pain, a pleasure, a desire, or a pure frustration otherwise than by its affective character. Here the specific phenomenological content of everything that is an "impression" and everything whose internal phenomenality is affectivity as such can be discovered. Precisely in order to designate this trait, which is common to everything that is impressional, and to avoid the equivocity of the concept of sensibility, Husserl writes that to highlight this contrast with the informing character, "we choose for it the expression of hyletic data or material data" (Hua III 173/205; translation modified).

The violence of Husserlian phenomenology, which is all the more brutal since it is unconscious, is to interpret the impressional and the affective power of revelation always in terms of "its role in contrast with the informing character," which is to say as something in itself excluded from every intentionality but constituted by it. When affectivity is considered as revelatory from the phenomenological point of view, it does not carry out the work of revelation on its own; instead, it is revelatory to the extent that it participates in the general essence of consciousness and is intentional. Feeling is an act, an "act of feeling." As such, it constitutes a specific affective layer that is "superposed on the stratum of the sensuous predicates, the stratum, that is, of the 'enjoyable,' of an object that is objectively 'sad,' of the 'beautiful,' the 'ugly,' etc." (Hua IV 15/16). Affectivity is revelatory insofar as it allows this object-oriented layer of the world to be seen. In a footnote that follows, Husserl comments: "The term 'predicates of feeling' has been referring to determining predicates of objects" (Hua IV 15/17). Yet, these objectively constituted affective predicates point back to a founding affectivity, and it is in this sense that "they are also called, quite legitimately, 'subjective,' as being predicates which in their very sense refer back to valuing subjects and their valuing acts" (ibid.). The founding affectivity is an intentional activity that constitutes axiological predicates, as Husserl explains, "*if we attribute objectivities to all intentional experiences, including affective lived experiences, objectivities toward which these lived experiences take a position in the mode of feelings, i.e. objects under the headings of value objects, practical objects, etc.*" (Hua IV 15/17). But what is the affective character of the act itself, of the mental process (*vécu*) of feeling? Husserl can only describe this by transferring the noetic-noematic schema of constitution onto it.

An intention necessarily precedes the experience of the feeling. The experience will "fulfill" and give itself to the intention, just as the intuitive content of the perception comes to fulfill the perceptual intention. Feeling is itself an intuitive content. Take, for example, a pleasure. Its experience is fulfilled literally like that of a perception. In the domain of feeling, the value-reception (*Wertnehmen*) is the analogue of perception (*Wahrnehmung*). Husserl writes: "Thus in the sphere of feelings what is meant by this talk of delighting is precisely that feeling in which the Ego lives with the consciousness of being in the presence of the object 'itself' in the manner of feelings. Just as there is, however, a sort of representing from afar, an empty representational intending outside which is not a being in the presence of the object, so there is a feeling which relates to the object emptily; and as the former is fulfilled in intuitive representing, so is the empty feeling fulfilled by way of the delighting" (Hua IV 9/11).

"Phenomenology" can thus be understood in two senses. In a naïve and pre-critical sense, it concerns a faithful description of the "phenomena," freed from every interpretation and every transcendent construction. Phenomenology, which is commonly understood in this way, can be divided into a number of particular investigations in accordance with the domains being studied. However, to describe the phenomena themselves, even in these particular domains, is to describe them as they are given and consequently in their givenness itself. It is to take this givenness into view and to thematize it. The object of phenomenology in the philosophical sense is never constituted by phenomena in the ordinary sense of the word; instead, the object of phenomenology is their phenomenality, and more precisely, the original mode by which this pure phenomenality becomes a phenomenon. The object of phenomenology, "the object in its How," in the how of its givenness, is this how as such.

Within the flow of phenomenological being, §85 of *Ideas I* distinguishes between a material layer and a noetic layer. "Hyletic phenomenology" has to do with the material element, while "noetic phenomenology" is related to the noetic moments. Between these two phenomenologies, there emerges a remarkable disproportion. Husserl observes: "The incomparably more important and richer analyses are found on the side of the noetic" (Hua III 175/207). And later he adds, "it (the hyletic) obviously stands far below the noetic and functional phenomenology" (Hua III 178/210). §86, which is engaged in "functional problems" pertaining to the "constitution of conscious-objectivities," explains why this is the case: "the noeses . . . by animating matter and combining it into the manifold-unitary continua and syntheses bring about consciousness of something" (Hua III 176/207). The aim of noetic phenomenology is *the establishment and promotion of pure phenomenality*, understood in terms of "the consciousness of something," as intentionality. What makes it "phenomenology" in the true sense is that its object is givenness as such, appearing in the philosophical sense, in the sense of the appearing of everything that appears. Because this appearing is concentrated in and only in intentionality, and because intentionality alone completes the work of manifestation, everything that is not intentional is dispossessed of this function. As non-intentional, we have seen that matter is delivered into the obscurity of beings. The hyletic, which deals with matter, is not only situated "far below noetic and functional phenomenology" (Hua III 178/210). It is not simply "subordinated" to it. To the extent that it only has a signification "by the fact that it provides possible gussets in the intentional eave, possible matter for intentive formations," a content for appearing and for the givenness that is the business of intentional phenomenology, hyletic phenomenology is a phenomenology in the trivial and pre-critical sense of the term (Hua III 178/210). It is not a true phenomenology.

All phenomenology is transcendental, insofar as it takes into consideration the givenness in which every experience is rooted. The reduction returns us to this original domain and, as Husserl notes, is transcendental:

> The characterization of the phenomenological reduction and, likewise, of the pure sphere of mental processes as "transcendental" rests

precisely on the fact that we discover in this reduction an absolute sphere of matter and noetic forms whose determinately structured combinations possess, according to immanent eidetic necessity, the marvelous consciousness of something determinate and determinable, given thus and so, which is something over against consciousness itself, something fundamentally other, non-really inherent [*Irreelles*], transcendent. (Hua III 204/239)

But this "immanent eidetic necessity" through which the "marvelous consciousness of something" emerges is intentionality; matter lacks this "property." "The determinately structured combinations" of "noetic matter and form" imply anything but the immanent eidetic necessity of intentionality; they imply that the appearing of intentionality requires something else besides the irreal exteriority onto which it opens; it requires a content, a matter, with which it can "combine." This material content is not just anything, a manifold of any kind whatsoever. It carries an essential trait within itself: it is the non-intentional and at the same time—without here explaining why—the impressional and the affective.

Intentional phenomenology is transcendental phenomenology, but the transcendental reduced to the intentional noesis is not truly a transcendental, an *a priori* condition of all possible experience, if it always requires what is wholly other than itself: the sensation, the impression. The latter must first be given in order for any experience whatsoever to take place. The thing, thought according to the presuppositions of intentionality, is the transcendent thing, the irreal, but it must first be something else that is neither irreal nor transcendent, something purely subjective and radically immanent. Everything given to us is constituted, in short, represented. But the constituted is, first of all, necessarily nonconstituted. Everything is transcendent but the transcendent itself is first of all nontranscendent. Everything that is given is given to us, so to speak, two times. The first givenness, the *Empfindung*, is mysterious. It is the type of givenness and given in which the mode of givenness is itself the given. Affectivity is both the impression's mode of givenness and its impressional content. It is the transcendental in a radical and autonomous sense. And then, this first given, which is always already given and presupposed, is given a second time in and through intentionality, as a transcendent and irreal thing, as its "vis-à-vis." "Transcendental" phenomenology, as intentional, is limited to the description of this second givenness, to the analysis of its essential modes and the various types of noeses and noemas corresponding to it. But it has set aside what it constantly presupposes, the first givenness. In its fleeting existence, hyletic phenomenology thinks and thematizes this first givenness as "sense data," which are understood in their "role" of providing a "matter" for noetic constitution and are thus presupposed by it.

According to §86 of *Ideas I*, hyletic phenomenology does not merely have a functional significance through which "it is subordinated to the phenomenology of transcendental consciousness. In addition, it has the characteristic of a self-contained discipline; as a self-contained discipline it 'has a value in itself'" (Hua III 178/210). What could this "value" be? Would this not make it possible to restore the hyletic's dignity as a properly phenomenological discipline? This could be done on one condition: that the consideration of matter enter into a reflection on the mode of givenness of things, that is, on "objects in their how." This is precisely the case, because the objects of transcendent perception are given to us only through their sensuous appearances, in such a manner that these data play a founding role for the givenness of every perceived object. It should not only be said that subjective adumbrations provide the matter for the constituting activities of intentional noeses. The direction of this proposition can also be reversed, since the constitutive noeses can function only by regulating themselves to the manner and the order in which these appearances are presented. Thus *hyle* is not merely a blind content for a noetic act that would inform it at its will. The impressional matters dictate the modalities of their own fulfillment to the noeses, in accordance with the play of their appearing. To put it otherwise, instead of functioning as a free principle for displaying the object, intentionality is drawn from the object, or rather from the matter from which the object proceeds, from the elements and the material components that will make the object into what it is. This determination goes so far as to imply that *hyle* even prescribes to *morphe* the essential modalities that it must adopt in the constitution of what it constitutes: perception, imagination, and memory. If one must consider the object not in its objective condition but in its own individual being, *hyle* is more essential than *morphe* for the determination of the object. By putting all transcendent apperceptions and thus all mundane objects out of play, is not the phenomenological reduction's explicit theme to lead back to the "phenomenon" and to what is given first and most truly in it?

However, in order for the hyletic to be able to reclaim the title of "phenomenology" by offering a decisive contribution to the question of givenness, this question immediately can be turned back onto hyletic phenomenology and this time in a way that no longer can warrant any further delay. Inasmuch as the givenness of things is accomplished through the mediation of sense data, one must know how they, in turn, are given. We have shown that there is no answer to this central question in *Ideas I*. Yet one cannot forget the explicit limitation of the problem at this stage of its elaboration in which Husserl takes "mental processes (*vécus*) as they offer themselves as unitary temporal processes in reflection on what is immanent" (Hua III 171/203). It is in the reflective attitude, in a phenomenological situation dominated by intentionality, that the impressional appeared as a content and as a datum, instead of perceiving in it the Archi-givenness as self-givenness, self-impression, and transcendental affectivity, which turned it into something impressional.[4] To the contrary, in the light of transcendence, under the gaze of reflection, and deprived of the essence that reigns in it and altogether determines it, this impressionality is nothing more than a content, that is, a datum whose givenness is derived this time from intentionality. Its impressional character (the shadow cast over its original essence through the representation of its essence in the truth) is nothing more than an empirical characteristic—something contingent, noticed and learned by experience. It is the *a posteriori* of all the philosophies that situate the *a priori* in any type of "I think" in which I represent myself, even if this contingent *a posteriori* is what is the most necessary to them.

The undeniable devaluation of the concept of *hyle* (and jointly of hyletic phenomenology) that becomes clear in the few pages devoted to it in *Ideas I* is due to the situation that we just evoked. The intentionality that lets something be seen also takes on the function of rationality. Letting something be seen is letting it be seen as something. It is to reveal the being of what one shows and to say what it is; it is to give it a sense. Intentional consciousness is equally a consciousness that gives sense. In contrast with that which gives and constructs the light of intelligibility, there stands that which is submitted to it in order for its being to be clarified and recognized through it. The material and sensuous contents, among others, are outside of this signifying information. For Husserl, they would only be "'psychic complexes,' for 'contents' fused together, for 'bundles' or 'streams' of sensations which, without sense in themselves, also cannot lend any 'sense' to whatever mixture" (Hua III 176/207–208). Husserl adds, "as content-complexes which merely exist without signifying anything" (Hua III 178/209). "Consciousness," declares Husserl again, "is therefore *toto coelo* different from what sensualism alone will see, from what in fact is irrational stuff without sense" (Hua III 176/208).

Yet the signifying information of nonsignifying material contents can only constitute the progressive rationalization of experience and its possibility, if this is indeed possible, as a concordant and unitary experience. If "a complex multiplicity of hyletic data, e.g. color-data, etc., acquire the function of a manifold adumbration of one and the same objective physical thing," it is because these data are presented in a certain way, as the adumbrations precisely of one single and same thing, it is because their appearing obeys an organization on which the synthetic unities and the objective order itself are modeled and based (Hua III 206/241–242). Whatever freedom one may recognize in noetic acts of sense-bestowal, a freedom with respect to which "the same material complex can undergo a diversity of mutually discrete and shifting construings," this freedom remains bound to a more profound necessity that is rooted in the subjectivity to which the reduction returns. This is precisely the lawfulness that is immanent to hyletic contents and according to which the constitution of a coherent and meaningful universe becomes possible (Hua III 206/242). This lawfulness is nothing other than the lawfulness of their givenness. We are sent back to this givenness twice: first, one must understand the ultimate possibility of every objective constitution; second, one must understand whether the ultimate givens, the hyletic givens by which the world is given, must themselves be given. Matter leads back to the question of its self-givenness, to the question of knowing whether this Archi-givenness is carried out by itself and thus autonomously. In short, it leads back to the question of whether the impression reveals itself as it is or whether, once more, it returns to the only mode of manifestation Western thought has recognized: the first ek-stasis of the outside and the ek-static dimension of phenomenality—intentionality is only one name for this opening.

The overcoming of the problematic of *Ideas I*, which limits itself to considering only mental processes and consequently hyletic mental processes, "as they offer themselves as unitary temporal processes in reflection on what is immanent," can be described as the necessity of "descending into the obscure depths of the ultimate consciousness which constitutes all such temporality" (Hua III 171/203). If the sensuous and impressional data should not be taken naively as mere "contents" that are simply "there" and if it is a matter of interrogating their givenness and the phenomenalization of the impression as such, one must turn to the consciousness that originally constitutes time. The constitution of time, as immanent phenomenological time, is the original constitution that constitutes all of the subjective elements whereby the world and its time are constituted in turn. It is the archi-constitution that carries out the archi-givenness.

This means that *the Archi-givenness is an archi-constitution; it is the archi-constitution of time.* Temporality is the archi-ek-stasis that constitutes the archi-phenomenality. Archi-givenness as archi-constitution, as the archi-ek-stasis of time, involves the impression, *hyle*. It is its own givenness, its self-givenness to itself, in such a manner that this givenness is not the impression itself but the givenness of the Archi-intentionalities that compose the archi-ek-stasis of time and in such a way that this givenness is not a self-givenness. What gives is not the impression itself but archi-intentionality; what is given is not and cannot be the impression either. When in order to be realized, and precisely because it is unable to do to so itself, the phenomenology of *hyle* is diverted into a phenomenology of intentionality, even of the archi-intentionality, it is thrown into an insurmountable aporia. It is unable to explain either the being of the impression or its givenness. It is in the *Lectures on the Internal Consciousness of Time* (1905) that, for the first and last time, phenomenology attempts to elucidate the givenness of the impression in a rigorous way. In this extraordinary text, which is certainly the most beautiful of twentieth-century philosophy, there is a huge confrontation in which a hyletic phenomenology in the radical sense of the term attempts to clear a path through the sediment of the tradition. This struggle results in a remarkably profound philosophy of archi-constitution that renews many of the aspects of classical thought yet does so at the cost of losing the essential and hyletic phenomenology itself.

Before witnessing this struggle and the philosophical death of life, one remark needs to be made concerning the prior development of phenomenology. Because it carries the essence of life within it, the impression adheres to everything that is alive and thereby to the whole world. In order to be absorbed in constitutive and functional problems, intentional phenomenology nonetheless constantly runs up against a matter that goes without any apprehension, not even the most transcendent one. The more the analysis works back toward the archaic forms of constitution, the more this material element both concerns and controls it. This is how it goes for what can be called the fundamental phenomenologies, such as those of the body or the ego. What then comes to falsify these investigations and to take them outside of their proper domain is that, in spite of the increasing role given to the impression, the impression does not truly guide the analysis and is never the actual nature of the experience being elucidated.

Every experience is first and foremost its own coming into experience, an initial indication to which everything that shows itself owes its nature, its laws, and ultimately what it is. For, what takes place in these phenomenologies is that the impression cannot be the determining principle of experience, precisely because it does not bring its phenomenological essence to experience, namely, the phenomenality of all the phenomena that make it up. And the impression is not the principle for all the experiences marked with the stamp of sensibility or affectivity, because *it is not the determining principle for itself.* Impressionability does not determine, in its irreducible phenomenological materiality, the impression's own arrival into being and thus does not determine the arrival of any of the experiences that rest on it. The original being of the impression has been broken, split up, and cast off into a primal exteriority and into a foreground of light in which it is exposed and exhibited. This is because this exposure and the work of ek-stasis are the condition for the impression's arrival into experience and for its first arrival to itself as a phenomenon, as a "sensible appearance." In place of the impression, Husserlian phenomenology would recognize only its constituted being, its being given to intentionality or to a proto-intentionality. When hyletic phenomenology is confronted with its own object, it is diverted into a phenomenology of constitution, and the main problems of the body, the ego, and the like are reduced to "constitutive problems," as in *Ideas II*. But, it is with respect to time, precisely when it is sunken into the "depths" of the archiconstitution and faced with the Impression, that Husserlian phenomenology will experience its most spectacular, significant, and decisive setback.

All things considered, the problem of self-givenness does not concern the impression alone. In a phenomenology of intentionality, intentionality carries out the original function of showing, which gives something to be seen. But a radical phenomenological thought must interrogate the manner in which the transcendental power, which gives every thing, is itself given. It is given to itself inasmuch as nothing but itself is at play here. Every actual and potential phenomenality first becomes a phenomenon, and it is only on the condition of a prior realized and given phenomenality that any phenomenon whatsoever can be become a phenomenon in it. The self-givenness of intentionality is a question that Husserlian phenomenology did not totally evade. It was even, without a doubt, its main preoccupation until its inability to respond to it and the ensuing boredom pushed it back into the shadows in which it continued to exist in the form of a secret obsession. For it is in the 1905 lectures that the central project of all phenomenology emerged, which was taken up with obstinacy and gave rise to repeated attempts and efforts. If this text is the most beautiful of phenomenology, it is because of this ultimate ambition. Although it becomes explicit sometimes in abrupt statements, there surfaces the unheard-of affirmation that the impression gives the principle that allows every thing to be seen and originally reveals intentionality to itself.

This is a strange situation in which one recognizes an inversion of the form that dominates classical phenomenology. Here the relation between form and matter is reversed. Because the impression is ultimately no longer the given but giving, the hyletic is possible and necessary, no longer as a discipline annexed to the ontic order and subordinated to a transcendental intentional phenomenology, but as a phenomenology and, moreover, as phenomenology itself. The thesis that *consciousness is impressional* has and must have an absolutely general scope. It does not simply signify that, without knowing why, consciousness is always affected impressionally, but that the impression, or to put it better, impressionality, constitutes consciousness itself. That is to say that impressionality is pure phenomenality as such, the matter and the phenomenological substance from which consciousness is made and thus the original phenomenality of all phenomena. This is why every objectivity, even the most transcendent one, is clothed with an affective predicative layer that is constituted by a specific intentionality, an "act of feeling." This is why the being, which is in itself nonaffective and nonsensible, is also clothed with properties that are in principle heterogeneous to it and that for this reason appear as additions, superimposed strata, that are determined by the tone of sensible and axiological "predicates." This is why the cosmos or nature has its flesh covered with large cuts and tears of emotional life. Everything that is and can possibly be must be given where the ek-stasis is originally given to itself, that is, in the pathos of its auto-impression and in its impressionality.

The question of the impression crosses through the admirable *Lectures on Time* from beginning to end, not because they would be devoted to a specific problem in which sense contents would play a preponderate role but precisely because their guiding theme is, under the heading of "the consciousness of internal time," first givenness. Consciousness is not impressional owing to any extrinsic determination, for example, a mysterious link with the body, because every extrinsic determination has been set aside by the phenomenological reduction, as it functions in this work. Instead, consciousness is impressional by its own nature, due solely to being conscious. This is why the impressionality of consciousness is affirmed with respect to all of its modalities, notably, even its intellectual modalities. For example, Husserl states that "a judging consciousness of a mathematical state of affairs is an impression" (Hua X 95/100) and likewise that "belief is actual belief, is an impression" (Hua X 103/109). It is an impression precisely in the way its originary being is initially and immediately experienced, prior to every apprehension of it that would be directed toward it and that would lead it to be perceived and considered as a psychic state. Husserl observes: "This belief in itself, or the sensation of belief, is to be distinguished from the act of belief in apprehension as my state, my act of judgment" (ibid.).

Why doesn't the thesis of impressional consciousness open onto a material phenomenology in the radical sense? The answer to this question allows us to understand not only the carrying over of the later developments of noetic and intentional phenomenology from its privileged beginnings but also these beginnings themselves, the first steps of the problem toward "pure hyletic givens." The reduction first established their indubitability because everything that exceeds what is actually sensed has been excluded, for example, the sonorous impression that is really heard. Every transcendent apprehension of an object situated beyond its subjective appearances, whose duration could not be confused with the duration of these "immanent" impressions (which would still last even when these impressions would be interrupted) has been excluded. The elucidated theme here is the pure hyletic given as it is actually experienced, actually sensed, actually understood and actually given. This shows that the reduction is carried out as a return to givenness and its how, to the how of its full realization and actuality. It is only in the how of the givenness that the given is actually given. What then is the givenness with which the reduction ends? What is the how of its actual fulfillment and full realization, if not the impression or the impressional as such? For it is precisely as pure impression and pure sensibility—which brackets everything that is heterogeneous to it, everything which would be other and from another order—that the hyletic given taken in the purity of its impressionality is truly an impression.

It suffices to read the first paragraphs of the *Lectures* to perceive that, in Husserl's eyes at least, there is none of this. The impression is not given as impressional; the sensed is not given as sensed, in and through its self-sensing. Instead, impressions are present in a consciousness of the now, a consciousness of the present baptized as "originary consciousness," originary perception, internal perception, immanent perception, originary sensing, internal consciousness, internal consciousness of time, and so forth. Let us denounce, without further delay, the deep ambiguity of this "originary" consciousness. It is partly an impression in the sense that the first givenness is surely inseparable from the impression, such that "consciousness is nothing without impression" (Hua X 100/106). But in this impression it is not the impression in and of itself, in its own affective flesh, so to speak, that accomplishes givenness; instead, it is an originary consciousness that gives it as being there now, as present. An originary perception gives it as being there, as really being there, and as being there now. To give it as really being there and as being there now is to confer this meaning onto whatever is given in this sort of consciousness. It is to let something be seen inasmuch as it is seen in this way, by conferring this meaning of being there, of really being there, as the present and the now. Intentionality is the type of consciousness that gives in this way and with this sense, that gives the first being as the first sense, as what is, and as what is now there.

The givenness of the impression, whose essence is the pure fact of being impressed as such, is stripped of its role in givenness in favor of an originary consciousness of the now. That is to say, in favor of what gives the now itself, which is perception in the Husserlian sense of what is given in its own being and "in flesh and bone." Thereafter, the essence of the impression is cast outside of being and into an irreality in which what gives it reality and an ontological weight has faded. But this paradox is only an apparent one. Inasmuch as reality resides in the self-experiencing of subjectivity and life, in the auto-impression of the impression, then it is only in this auto-impression and its own givenness that the reality of the impression and life can be given to me. Pain itself teaches me about pain and not some kind of intentional consciousness that would aim at its presence, its being there now. The second givenness, which is the ek-static givenness in the perception of the now, presupposes the first non-ek-static givenness in affectivity, so that the second givenness can never realize itself, for example, as an intentional perception of pain in the now. Instead, the second givenness presupposes its realization elsewhere in the affectivity and impressionality of pain. Here the equivocity of the Husserlian understanding of impressional consciousness, which continually confuses two types of givenness and surreptitiously gives one type the properties belonging to the other type, is undone.

With striking clarity, the context of the analysis brings out the fact that the originary consciousness of a sensation in its now does not give this sensation in the subjective reality of its being as it is impressionally given to itself; instead, it is discarded into an irreality where it can be represented but not experienced. A continually renewed but continually thwarted effort emerges to restore the constancy and being of that which in principle lacks it and that continually flows into nonbeing and into this noematic irreality in which all life is lost. This basic ontological impoverishment of the impression, even though it is given in the originary consciousness of the now, is expressed by the fact that, held in the now, it lets itself be carried away with it, falling like the now into the "having just passed" and then into "the further and further passed," continually distancing itself from the actual now to sink into an increasing and darkening obscurity, at the end of which it becomes "unconscious."

Modification is the process by which the now—and the impression given in it—continually changes into the past. It produces a continual sliding that carries everything away and slips away from itself at each point. There cannot be any fixed point, nothing escaping this flow, and *as a result, no true now*. The now "is always and essentially the borderpoint [*Randpunkt*] of an extent of time" (Hua X 70/72), just as "the present is a limit" (Hua X 69/71). This term, this limit, does not designate a portion of this flow, however small it may be, or a minimal zone that could be withdrawn from it as a moment or a really present given. Husserl claims that "no concrete part of the flow can make its appearance as nonflow" (Hua X 114/118). This is what makes the present only an "ideal limit." Precisely because it itself is flowing, the now-portion of the flow constitutes "the rough 'now': as soon as we divide this rough now further, it in turn immediately breaks down into a finer now and a past, and so on" (Hua X 40/42). But, this now is the impression. The auto-impression in each impression, which is the reality of absolute subjectivity as the essence of all reality and as the flesh of life, is reduced to a pure ideality in the intentional presentation of the now. Because of its infinite divisibility, this pure ideality is reduced in turn to a simple point that is likewise ideal. That is what destroys the consciousness of the now's ontological claim to be a perception, "an act originally giving reality," which gives reality in itself and as it truly is. At least, this is what happens in the case of the impression, which constitutes the substance and the stuff of every reality, regardless of whether it is understood in terms of subjectivity or nature.

This failure and ontological destruction of the originary consciousness of the now is what the entire development of the *Lectures* aims both to hide and avoid. If, in conformity with its nature, each point of the flow collapses in and with the consciousness of the now, it suffices then to realize the flow as such, to hypostasize it in some way, and to turn it into a quasi-substance for which this collapse will become a mode. It would *be a part in the sense in which a part is the part of a whole*, existing solely within it, finding its essence and basis within it, just as the whole is expressed and realized concretely in the sum of its parts. The theory of parts and wholes elaborated in the "Third Logical Investigation" comes to the rescue of the phenomenology of the impressional now, which is on the verge of failure. It authorizes the subterfuge by which the now as an ideal limit and a pure ideality can be transformed into a concrete phase of the flow, while the flow itself is transformed into a concrete reality, a real flow, namely, the flow of consciousness.[5] That is the ontological mystification that is the precondition for this entire analysis. The impression never "is" transcendent and never is given in itself in the ek-static presentation of the now. This ek-static presentation only gives the impression in order to dismiss its living impressional reality and to turn it into noematic irreality. The impression is interpreted as finding its original and ownmost being in this arrival in irreality, in this sliding into the no longer being of "having just passed."

Given that the impression in the consciousness of the now is reduced to its own sliding into the no longer being of the having just passed, *the unity of the consciousness of the now with the retention, which is the consciousness of the "having just passed," is ensured*. These two consciousnesses are joined in such a way that the former modifies constantly into the latter and that *this modification rules both of them in some way*. It ensures that the consciousness of the now is never merely a consciousness of the now but a consciousness of the now sliding into the past and thus, at the same time, a consciousness of the retention. The consciousness of the temporal extension goes from the now to the past and includes both of them within itself, as its limits or rather as its phases and parts. They have become as concrete as the whole in which they are inscribed and the extension for which they are the constitutive and real elements. This gives birth to the illusion of a homogenous, real, and concrete phenomenological flow. It would be composed of phases that only exist within the flow in such a way that each phase would refer to the other ones and would only be possible through them. There would be no now without its having just passed, and there would be no having just passed without a now to which it is constantly linked, as the having just passed of this now, or to put it better, as this now itself as just having passed. Husserl states: "a phase is conceivable only as a phase, without the possibility of extension. And the now-phase is conceivable only as the limit of a continuity of retentions, just as every retentional phase is itself conceivable only as a point belonging to such a continuum" (Hua X 33/35).

The problem of the homogeneity of this real and concrete phenomenological flow as well as its ontological status as a continuum can be made more precise, if we ask ourselves about the prior consciousnesses that constitute it. The impressional consciousness of the now and the retentional consciousness are not only joined to one another; they also complete one another to the point of exchanging their roles. The originary consciousness gives the impression as now in such a way that, when perceived in the regard of the now, the impression conceals its reality and slides into nonbeing. This sliding is precisely what the retention grasps. It is the consciousness of the collapse but in this collapse it retains the now of the impression, giving it as past and as no longer being. But, at least it does give the impression in this way and thus keeps it out of nothingness. The consciousness that gives real being originally in the present does not give the real. It does not give the reality of the impression but rather casts it away into irreality. The retention recuperates, to the extent that it can, the real being of the impression which is given in the now, as a being that has never been real nor really given in this now. The retention gives it *in the sense that it had really been given* and had been given in something that was a now. This extraordinary reversal of roles between the so-called originary consciousness, which cannot give reality at all, and the consciousness of the past, which at least gives reality in the past, explains the expanding role that retentions exert within the entirety of the flow. The retention turns the flow into what it is: a phenomenological given. It alone can ensure the cohesion of this whole, because each phase is joined to the others through trails of retentions or the "longitudinal intentionality" which is a retention spanning the entire flow.

This primacy of the retention explains the ontological reevaluation made of the object. The retention is an originary consciousness; it is a perception in the sense of an originally giving act, which is to say that it constitutes the sole possible means of access to what it gives. What it gives cannot be given in any other way than in and through this act. The retention is the intuition of the past. It is precisely because the flow is given in a retentional archi-constitution that it is not just a phenomenological flow but also a real flow. By returning the experience of the past as just having passed to an original consciousness, the polemic against Brentano (who, by contrast, reduced the past to the imaginary) puts the entirety of the flow back into the actuality of a true phenomenological given and thus into reality. And, inasmuch as the flow is the site in which sense data and hyletic givens appear, it is the impression or the impressional as such which seems once again to offer itself up to the ek-static exposure's power of showing.

The ontological reevaluation of the retention in fact has a strict phenomenological significance that Husserl expresses thus: "What I am conscious of retentionally is absolutely certain, as we have seen" (Hua X 49/51). The theoretical justification for this categorical assertion is locked in a paralogism that would denounce its pseudo-phenomenological character. It is not because the retention is absolutely certain that the flow is itself given with certainty; it is because this flow must be validated in its temporal extension—including the now that only exists as temporally extended through the flow—that the retention is invested with this radical phenomenological signification. Husserl explains: "If it belongs to the essence of a content given in perception that it is temporally extended, then the indubitability that pertains to perception can signify nothing other than indubitability with respect to temporally extended being" (Hua X 85/89). Husserl clearly perceives that this requirement implies nothing less than a redefinition of absolute subjectivity and its original mode of revelation to oneself, that is, a redefinition of the *cogito* itself; however, he only brushes this issue aside. Instead, he tries to resolve this issue through the mere reaffirmation of retentional indubitability: "It is clear that the much-discussed evidence pertaining to the perception of the internal, the evidence of the *cogito*, would lose all significance and sense if we were to exclude temporal extension from the sphere of evidence and true givenness" (Hua X 85/90).

Here arises one of the aporias of Husserlian phenomenology. Instead of being able to found temporal extension and thus the continuum of the phenomenological flow as a real and homogenous flow, the ontological and phenomenological reevaluation of the retention will break the continuum. From then on the consciousness of the now, instead of including the retentional extension that would grow like a "living horizon" within itself, is separated from the flow by an abyss. It is led back to the point where it dissolves into the ideality of something that is infinitely divisible. To be sure, one must not forget the phenomenological difference between different types of intentions that constitute the main thrust of phenomenology and have provided its most beautiful analyses. The consciousness of the now and the retention are both "originary consciousnesses"—they are both perceptions. Whatever they give, they give in itself and in its reality. What is given by these two types of consciousness is not real, however, in the same sense or in the same way. Consequently, it cannot be homogenous. Quite the contrary! The originary consciousness of the now gives being as being there now, that is, as something real. The retention is the originary consciousness of the past as past; it only gives what it gives as no longer being or as a nonbeing. As for the impression in its subjective, impressional and living reality, not one bit of its reality enters into the retention. Following Husserl's explicit dictates, "the retentional 'contents' are not at all contents in the original sense." He adds, "the retentional tone is not a present tone . . . it is not really on hand in the retentional consciousness" (Hua X 31/33).[6] Therefore, when the impressional consciousness of the present slides into retentional consciousness at each instant, being collapses into nothingness—at each instant. The proof of this is in the fact that at each instant being must be reborn *ex nihilo*. It is reborn in the form of a new now that wells up continually as "the living source-point of being, in the now" in which "an ever new primal being" finds its source, substituting itself for the one which has just faded into the past, into "what has just been" but yet is completely and totally in the past (Hua X 69/71).

This continual sinking of being into the abyss of a nothingness that continually opens up below it is what gives Husserlian description its fascinating, even hallucinatory character, as well as its incoherence and absurdity. The supposed phenomenological continuum of the flow is constantly broken. Its so-called homogenous reality, which makes it a whole, is broken into pieces. A radical and barely conceivable discontinuity, instead, is placed in between these pieces of being and nothingness that are exchanged constantly in a magical transubstantiation. It is as if one who stands on the crest of the now not only has one foot on the ground and the other in the void but also is continually falling from the ground and into the void, stumbling like a drunken man or like a person walking on a conveyor belt or an escalator in the wrong direction. While one places one's foot on the moving surface, it slips away behind oneself; then, quickly, another step is made in order not to fall down, but it too slips away. Our protagonist, off-balance like a marionette, continues on this jerky path, which does not advance.

The Husserlian analysis struggles with this ontological collapse, which continually breaks the continuum of the flow and makes this incoherent passage between being and nothingness. The most striking feature of this analysis is that it entrusts the task of assuring the return of being and its continual running off into an ever new now *not to this continuum but to the impression*, in which the essence of Being as an Archi-Revelation will be concentrated. The significance of this constant recourse to the impression—the great breakthroughs of these admirable lectures are rooted, if only in their virtual state, in this recourse—increases once its decisive phenomenological impact is recognized, because it dismisses intentional phenomenology and every ek-static mode of presentation, at least with respect to their claim to be originary. Let us begin with this latter point.

The phenomenology of time is a phenomenology of the impression that dismisses the impression's own power of revelation in order to entrust this power exclusively to ek-static givenness. The ek-static givenness of the impression is its presentation in the originary consciousness of the now, to which the retention and the protention are linked, such as the projection of the future (*avenir*) that is the pure fact of being to come (*à venir*). Together the consciousnesses of the now, the past, and the future constitute the unified structure of a triple ecstasy, which defines the how of every givenness of phenomena as Husserl conceives them. Husserl observes: "We have 'objects in the how' . . . the form of the how is the orientation: the now, the just past, the future" (Hua X 117/121; translation modified). But, as we have seen, givenness, understood in a general sense, cannot escape the question of self-givenness. One must understand how each actual, retentional, or protentional consciousness itself becomes a "phenomenon." One must also understand how the consciousness of internal time is a consciousness even before the phenomenological act of sense-bestowal that it carries out with the appearing of the now, the just passed, and the future, and thus the appearing of everything within the temporal extension of the immanent flow of internal time consciousness. To this crucial question about the most original phenomenality, which is the phenomenality of constituting as such, Husserl offers no other response than a restatement of the phenomenality of the constituted, that is, that each constitutive phase of the flow only comes into phenomenality to the extent that it is itself constituted. As such, the act of constituting never becomes a phenomenon and the ultimate constitutor thus remains "anonymous." This anonymity epitomizes the phenomenological failure of Husserlian phenomenology.

§39 of the *Lectures* is a poorly disguised confession of this failure. The objection that the manifestation of the flow of consciousness would require a second flow placed under it and be charged with the task of turning it into a phenomenon is resolved by the claim that the flow "constitutes its own unity," that it is both the appearing and what makes it appear (Hua X 80/84). Although this provides an account of the flow's own appearing, the claim concerning self-appearing (*Selbsterscheinung*) secretly splits into two. It includes, on one hand, the affirmation that the flow brings about its own manifestation. For example, each retention makes visible the phase that it retains and, through it, all the preceding phases and consequently all the past flowing of the flow. Thus it reveals the flow itself. But this thesis about self-givenness, which posits that the flow is both what gives and what is given, is still speculative. It implies another thesis, explicitly formulated elsewhere, that what is given by the flow is the flow itself, in person and in its own reality (*Selbst*). And this is what is false, if the original reality of the flow refers to all of the constituting phases, which are never given as such but only as constituted. Husserl therefore writes: "The constituting and the constituted coincide, and *yet naturally they cannot coincide in every respect*. The phases of the flow of consciousness in which phases of the same flow of consciousness become constituted phenomenally cannot be identical with these constituted phases, nor are they" (Hua X 83/88).

They are so little connected, indeed, that there is nothing in common between them but a radical ontological and phenomenological heterogeneity, which deepens itself forever between the coming forward in the light of ek-static phenomenality and that which ultimately ensures this arrival but yet never displays itself there. Because this nonarrival in the light of the ek-stasis is not just provisional but rather an essential impossibility, every analogy between what can be clarified by this light and what withdraws from it by principle, indeed every inference from the former to the latter, is absurd. Husserl claims: "Time-constituting phenomena, therefore, are evidently objectivities fundamentally different from those constituted in time," such that the predicates of the latter "cannot be meaningfully ascribed to them. Hence it also can make no sense to say of them (and to say with the same signification) that they exist in the now and did exist previously, that they succeed one another in time or are simultaneous with one another, and so on" (Hua X 74–75/79). Unfortunately, the rest of the text, including all the subsequent phenomenology and the unpublished manuscripts on the living present, will say the same thing. It will project the previous discourse concerning the constituted flow onto the phenomena constituting time, metaphorically making them too into a flow with its actual now point, its protentional and retentional phases, and so on. From then on, this flow is subject to the same aporias and to the same ontological collapse as the phenomenologically constituted flow that is called "immanent."

The inability of the ek-static givenness to become an essence as self-givenness is the unperceived but decisive motif that continually leads the *Lectures* from intentional analysis back to its hyletic sublayer. This is precisely a return from the originary consciousness of the now back to the impression without which this now would not exist. It is the reality of the impression in its original subjective reality—as an *Ur-impression*—that enables the now to exist. The now is the first representation in a noematic irreality of something that only "is" in and through its auto-affection. The now, no more than the retention, cannot hold or retain the impression within itself, because the impression was never held there. The impression is nothing that the intentional gaze, even the one directed toward the now, could ever grasp in its reality. Thus the aporia of the Husserlian conception of the phenomenological flow as a continuum of homogenous parts is already dissolved for us. This aporia held that the supposed continuum was broken at each instant by the ontological collapse of a now which was forced to be reborn at each instant. In light of the concept of reality that it puts forward, material phenomenology can provide a coherent theory of the ontological homogeneity of the "immanent" phenomenological flow. *This homogeneity is tied to the flow's irreality.* This is because the impression, taken as the now, the just passed or the coming to be, does not have its place in the flow. Its original subjectivity has never belonged there; instead, it belongs entirely outside of the ek-static dimension, in the radical Elsewhere that I am. But this remark is perhaps premature.

The return from the now back to the impression, and more precisely, to the originary impression, is the implicit or explicit content of the analyses of the *Lectures*. For example, in §31, which treats the problem of individuation, one can find a double movement. First, there is a movement which goes from the impression to the ek-static stroke of the now, which subordinates the impression to the ek-static and alone can endow the impression with the individualizing moment that will make it into what it is. If one considers a sensation that remains the same, for example, a prolonged *do*, it is different in this now here from its successive now. It is thus the sounding of the now that differentiates it at each time, that is to say, the ek-static form of time. To say that sensation is individualized by the now in which it is given is to make a claim about the characteristics of the ek-static regard and what appears in it. It is to give them as characteristics of being. It is to say that to be is to be what is there in front of this regard; it is what is there now.

However, the ek-static regard is as of yet only an empty form. What it gives is an empty space in which no impression is able to display its being or to appear in its own reality. Hence, there is a second movement in §31 leading from this empty place, which is indifferent to every real, determinate, and individual being and thus unable to grant individuation. It goes back to the essence that contains and produces them. Husserl writes: "The moment of the original temporal position is naturally nothing by itself; the individuation is nothing in addition to what has individuation" (Hua X 68/70). This dismissal of the ek-static present's claim to found individuality disqualifies its capacity to define the true present, namely, the Archi-Present situated in the Archi-Revelation by which each impression is an impression. Husserl continues: "But the now-point must, in strictness, be defined through original sensation" (Hua X 67/69). And, "Primal impression has as its content that which the word 'now' signifies, insofar as it is taken in the strictest sense" (Hua X 67/70). Being is founded through this Archi-Presence as the Archi-Revelation that brings itself about as the Impression. Husserl observes: "The primal impression is . . . the primal source of all further consciousness and being" (ibid.) Henceforth, the impression is written in the plural and is not grasped in its originarity, that is to say, in its essence. Instead, it is confused with what it makes possible, with the sensations constituted in the phenomenological flow. For example, Husserl writes, "the many primal sensations flow" (Hua X 77/81) or "the primal sensations that introduce the retentional process" (Hua X 78/83). This fact attests to the inability of Husserlian phenomenology to construct a true problem of the impression and impressional consciousness.

The same situation occurs in "Appendix VI." The hypostasis of the flowing of the phenomenological flow, which takes up indiscriminately both the constituting and the constituted, raises the question of knowing whether something escapes from this flow in which everything is flowing. The answer to this question is the form of the flow. The flow presents a fixed structure, a permanent form of the three ek-static components of the consciousness of internal time: actual, protentional, and retentional. Conforming to this structure, the phases of the flow sliding through it necessarily appear as future, present, and past phases, in such a way, however, that this fixed formal structure of the flow is still nothing on its own and does not determine any actual concrete flow. It requires a "content," and the impression is this content, which bears reality and makes the flow concrete. This surpassing of the ek-static form of the temporal flow toward something that is not ek-static is no sooner recognized by the Husserlian text than it is misrepresented by a crude parologism. Form is nothing without the content that, as the impressionality of the impression, is phenomenologically and ontologically heterogeneous to form. It is presented as being neither contingent nor heterogeneous in relation to form. To the contrary, content belongs to it and defines it because form requires the now and the now requires the impression. Because form alone does not result in any concrete experience without the originary impression, it follows that this originary impression takes over for the form and constitutes it! Here is a string of sophisms: "This constant form is always filled anew by 'content,' but the content is certainly not something introduced into the form from without. On the contrary, it is determined through the form of regularity—only in such a way that this regularity does not alone determine the concretum. *The form consists in this, that a now becomes constituted by means of an impression*" (Hua X 114/118). The passage that immediately follows shows that this appeal to the impression is not the opportunity for the phenomenology of ek-static temporality to free itself from its presuppositions, but only an opportunity to repeat them continually: "a trail of retentions and a horizon of protentions are attached to the impression. But this abiding form supports the consciousness of constant change, which is a primal fact: the consciousness of the change of impression into retention with a fresh impression continuously makes its appearance" (ibid.).

Why is the impression always there, again and again? We have begun to understand that this is because nothing ever comes into being without first being embraced in the pathos of its original Parousia. Because the origin is a pathos and because, as such, this pathos is always real, nothing ever comes into being except as an impression. For this reason, the impression "is always there." This is what the ek-static regard perceives before itself as "an ever-present now," taking on the form of an always new impression. It perceives this without being able to understand it, because it exists on the level of an astonishing and contingent fact but not that of apodicticity. But, to perceive the impression before oneself without questioning further into what makes it possible, into what makes the impression in general possible, and into what makes its extension to the whole of being necessary, is to fail to recognize its essence and to misrepresent its key features.

This misrepresentation functions in two ways. The first, which we have already described, involves the substitution of the impression's original being with its constituted being, and *this substitution is carried out as soon as the hyletic given is considered within the phenomenological flow*. This is not only the case in *Ideas I* but also in the *Lectures*. Thereafter, the ek-static givenness of the impression in the consciousness of internal time replaces its self-givenness in impressionality, and the question of the impression is lost from sight. This obsession is visible in the problem of the originary impression (*Ur-impression*). The original character of the *Ur-impression* does not refer to the arrival of the impression as such but to its appearing within the flow at the constituted now-point, as the impression that provides the "content" for a form. This fall of the impression into the constituted being of the flow is a common trait of Husserlian phenomenology that perverts it from beginning to end. The brilliant insight of the lectures, let us recall, was that every act and every lived experience is an impression. As Husserl puts it: "In a certain sense, therefore, all experiences are intended through impressions or are impressed" (Hua X 89/93). However, the impression that constitutes the being of every act and mental process (*vécu*), in which this act and this mental process are given, is itself "an immanent present." It is an immanent given in the Husserlian sense of an appearance in the duration of the phenomenologically constituted flow. To say that it is constituted by the consciousness of internal time is to say that it is revealed in and through the ek-static structure of temporality. So subjectivity would be designated as ultimately impressional only then to be taken outside of its own being, cast off into the archi-forms of the temporal ek-stasis where its essence is lost. It has become a world, a first world, an "inner world"—all that it never truly is.

Its being, which is always held in the pathetic embrace of its original Parousia and is possible only in this immanence, has been absolutely exploded. Its fragments have been dismantled and dispersed into an incredible puzzle. Henceforth, it is offered up to the work of an analysis that will pick up the pieces on the basis of false presuppositions. This announces the great crisis of the modern subject, which follows from the pure and simple ignorance about its essence and about the impression as well.

The misrepresentation of the impression's original being in terms of its constituted being points back to a deeper falsification whereby the structure of ek-static temporality is inserted into the impression itself in order to define its essence in terms of this structure. This falsification is both the cause and effect of the reduction of the impression's original being to its constituted being. This falsification has this effect because it is clear that the impression's being was inserted into the temporality of the phenomenological flow as an immanent content, a "hyletic given," a "sensible appearing," and so on. Having become a fragment of the flow, this content carries within itself the feature that the flow imposes on each one of its phases, namely, that of referring protentionally and retentionally to all of the others. Hence, Husserl can and must claim: "As far as the single sensation is concerned, it is in fact nothing single. That is to say, primary contents are at all times bearers of rays of apprehension and they do not occur without such rays" (Hua X 105/110). And more explicitly: "Every sensation has its intentions that lead from the now to a new now" (Hua X 105/111).

However, it is not only as constituted in the flow that the impression is shot through with the upsurge of the future, but also within itself, in its own essence. "But the regard from the now towards the new now, this transition, is something original . . . I said that this belongs to the essence of perception; *I would do better to say that it belongs to the essence of impression*" (Hua X 107/112). This radical falsification of the impression's own essence reduces it to essence of the first perception, which is the ek-static perception of phenomenological temporality. This falsification has its source in a prior production of the impression, under the regard of this perception, as a primary content in the flow. That is what the passage goes on to make clear: "It is certainly true of every 'primary content,' of every sensation" (ibid.).

But perhaps the impression was only reduced to its ek-static appearing in immanent temporality because this mode of presentation is the only one that phenomenology knows, such that the recourse to the impression in order to assure the ultimate givenness as a self-givenness was conceivable only by this surreptitious insertion of intentionality's power of showing into non-intentional matter. Only on that condition alone could sensation have been situated at the heart of subjectivity and assigned the task of ensuring its ultimate function in subjectivity. The text we are discussing ends with some extraordinary definitions of sensation, because they exclude the entire impressional element from sensation. They exclude everything that would make it a true "sensation" by identifying it purely and simply with the consciousness that constitutes time. Husserl defines sensation in the following ways: "We regard sensing as the original consciousness of time; in it an immanent unity such as color or sound, an immanent unity such as a wish or pleasure, and so on, becomes constituted" (ibid.). And again: "Sensation is presenting time-consciousness" (ibid.). But when sensation itself becomes the ek-static gaze, the impressional and the sensible as such have ceased to belong to it. They are no longer anything but contents placed before it whose sensible and affective character remains an enigma—and likewise the affective and sensible characteristics that one continues to identify in the name of sensing. Passages such as the following one are the overwhelming testimony of the disastrous dismemberment of sensation into a form and a content, each of which are nonsensible. This dismemberment is the internal essence of the impression: "a sensuous content, for example—say, sensed red. Sensation here is nothing other than the internal consciousness of the content of sensation. The sensation red (as the sensing of red)" (Hua X 127/131).

The genius of Husserl is that he more than any other philosopher is aware of the internal difficulties of his thought. In the presence of the hypostasis of the ek-static consciousness of time and the exclusive reign of the modification that produces the continuous flow and gnaws away at the present by reducing it to an ideal limit, it is this unrivaled clear-sightedness that prompts Husserl to ask about the beginning phase of a mental process: "Does it also come to be given only on the basis of retention, and would it be "unconscious" if no retention were to follow it?" (Hua X 119/123). This would be, Husserl understands, to put all of our life in the past. For this reason, Husserl makes the following categorical claims: "It is just nonsense to talk about an 'unconscious' content that would only subsequently become conscious. Consciousness is necessarily *consciousness* in each of its phases" (ibid.). The inevitable reevaluation of the present that such declarations call for, however, does not result in any positive definition of a now that would be capable of tearing itself away from the evanescence of the flow. This is because the consciousness of the now remains ek-static and thus does not have a hold on the impression's original being, which is a subjectum and a subsistent basis for all reality.

This can be seen clearly in the parallel between the consciousness of the now and the retention. Even if they only aim thematically at their objects and can be called nonobjective in this sense, nonetheless they are both intentional. And this is the reason why Husserl can compare the consciousness of the now to the retention: "Just as the retentional phase is conscious of the preceding phase without making it into an object, so too the primal datum is already intended—specifically, in the original form of the 'now'—without its being something objective" (ibid.).

The question of the nonmodified, as the antecedent prerequisite of every retention and thus of the flow itself, is what is at stake. What is there in the flow that is not modified? It cannot be the form of the flow alone, because it is empty and it repeats itself at each now only to fall into the abyss. The fixed form of the flow and its continuous flowing are reciprocal; nothing subsists in them but nonsubsistence, slippage, and disappearance. It is necessary to realize that there is no real life in the flow; there is no life in the present; no life is possible there. What remains, then, through the modifications as absolutely unmodified, as this unmodified subjectum that carries in it and defines an element of reality, as something that, never being carried away by the flow, subsists, as the absolute being that we call the Present, as the eternal present of Life, and as its living Present? Life is that by which there is a reality and, for this reason, never ceases. In the impression, it is that by which there is an impression, the silent embrace in which it experiences and senses itself at each moment of its being, without ever getting rid of itself and without the gap of any distance that would ever separate it from itself.

But does not the impression constantly change? Indeed, it does. Yet what never changes and never breaks away is what makes it an impression; this is the essence of life. Like the Euripus Strait, life is changing, but yet through its variations it does not cease to be Life in an absolute sense. It is the same Life, the same experience of the self that does not cease to experience itself, to be absolutely the same, one single and same Self. When we say that life changes or that the self is transformed, we mean the following: what this self-experience experiences is modified, but in this modification it does not cease to experience itself and that is what, in spite of this change, does not change. What is it that is not modified in impressional life, where one continually undergoes new impressions in such a way that there is always a new impression there? Apparently the impression to come is and will be an impression. What is always already there before it and what remains after it, is what is necessary for its arrival. This is not the empty form of an "I think" or the ek-static gaze of the future but the radical auto-affection of life in its phenomenological reality. Every "new impression" is only one of its modalities. As for our life, there is never any sort of absolute now, which would then fall into the past; there is only this life, which is always changing and yet always the same. So are we not like some sort of hapless clown who has one foot in being and the other one in nothingness?

"When the primal sensation," Husserl writes, "recedes and is continuously modified" (Hua X 79/83). When the primal sensation recedes, there is something that does not recede. This is, we have said, its essence as the auto-affection of life. What remains is thus not like an unchanging substance within the universal flow, like a rock at the bottom of the river; it is the historicity of the absolute, the eternal arrival of life to itself. Because this arrival does not cease to come, what remains is change. This change is not a dehiscence and an escape from the self at every instant; instead, it is what in the experience of the self and in the implosion of this experience, arrives in the self, takes hold of the self, and increases through its own being. What remains is growth. Growth is the movement of life that is realized out in life in virtue of what it is—its own *subjectivity*.

Husserl sought to think the movement of life and did so in magnificent terms: "The waking [*wache*] consciousness, the waking life, is a living-towards [*Entgegenleben*], a living that goes from the now towards the new now" (Hua X 106/112). This passage, the text adds, "is something original" (ibid.). The movement of life is a drive that throws it constantly into "a living-toward." This living-toward cannot be anything but the original revelation of being to itself, or, life. Husserl does not think about the movement of life by starting from the essence of life as something identical to itself; instead, he starts from the only mode of manifestation that he knows: an ek-stasis and the protention of the future. Thereby the movement of life is totally falsified. It is no longer *the drive, which is born from life in its struggle with itself* and from life driven back against itself and overwhelmed by itself. Such a life can no longer maintain itself in the suffering of its suffering of itself; it *aspires to change itself*, to become other. Aspiring to become other should not be taken in the sense of becoming something outside of oneself, but of changing this suffering into an enjoyment, into the self-enjoyment of one's own essence. Thought from the starting point of ek-stasis and the ek-static, the movement of life is no longer what it always is: *a force*. That is to say the force situated in this primordial embrace of the self, where every power, every possibility of taking, grasping, embracing, and even the body is rooted. Instead, for Husserl the movement of life became the movement of a regard: "It belongs to the essence of perception not only that it has in view a punctual now and not only that it releases from its view something that has just been, while 'still-intending' it in the original mode of the 'just-having-been,' but also that it passes over from now to now and, in anticipation, goes to meet the new now" (Hua X 106/112).

What comes to us in the ek-stasis of the regard continually has its place outside of us. When it slides from the future to the present, this present is "a punctual now in view." As such, it is never what we are but that from which we are forever separated: the distance of exteriority. Thus the movement of life is distorted a second time, because it is no longer the force of a drive. What it wants is no longer the satisfaction of the drive, which is what life desires as a self and as a part of itself, as its self-transformation through its self-expansion, as a truth that is its own flesh and the substance of its joy, and which is the Impression. Having become an intentional consciousness and objective thought, the movement of life can only seek to modify this stream of images that flows from the future to past or to master a play of representations. The entirety of life, from beginning to end, is perverted and its sense lost when one does not see that it is always the force of feeling that throws life into living-toward. And what it lives-toward is always life as well. It is the intensification and the growth of its power and pathos to the point of excess.

A fragment from the lectures was able to call into question this metaphysics of representation, which condemns modern thought as well as its past. According to "Appendix I," each primal impression is constantly modified, the modification that results from this modification of the primal impression is modified in its turn, and so on to infinity. Thus there is a "continuous production of modifications of modifications," which is none other than "the time-constituting continuum" (Hua X 100/106). For, at the heart of this continuum, a decisive split emerges between the primal impression on one hand and the continuous production of modifications on the other. This distinction arises from the production of modifications' being taken in the strict sense of the word. It is a real production that is the feat of consciousness and owes everything to it, whereas the continual upsurge of the originary impression escapes from this production of modifications by consciousness and owes it nothing. Husserl notes: "The primal impression is the absolute beginning of this production, the primal source, that from which everything else is continuously produced. But it itself is not produced; it does not arise as something produced " (ibid.). The continual retentional modification, the Ek-stasis, is produced, while the impression is not. This is not a difference that is external to their being; instead, being in its own essence is in question. The production of ek-stasis means that ek-stasis itself is production; it is in fact the upsurge of the ek-static dimension. To be sure, this production should not be confused with an explicit act of the I, like the gaze of a specific intentionality. For it is only if this production has taken place and previously established this dimension that a conscious gaze can aim at something as the future, present, or past. This is what Husserl means when he refers to the intentions that constitute internal time consciousness as being essentially passive, as already having been fulfilled, prior to every possible expectation, every consciousness of the present and memory. This is the reason why we have called the ek-static constitution of time an archi-constitution.

What is produced in these absolutely passive syntheses of time consciousness is nonetheless a production, and with the opening of the dimension of time, it produces a field of play for the acts of consciousness and the I. Insofar as the passivity of the primal impression differs from the production of modifications, nothing of this sort occurs. Nothing belonging to this production is produced. It is not the purely passive and relentless advent of an ek-stasis, instead this is insurmountably excluded from the self. Here passivity as nonproduction means the irremissible, unsurpassable, and uninfringable embrace of life with itself. In this embrace, there is no separation because the how of life's givenness to itself is neither ek-stasis nor its endless production. This passivity is in fact completely foreign to it. The impression signifies suffering as the suffering of oneself at each point of one's living being. This is also the reason why the continuum belonging to the impression has nothing to do with the continuum of modifications. The latter are only the iteration of the ek-static rupture, while the former are what, placed below it or rather within it, supports it and makes it possible at each moment. This continuum is the continuum of life—its embrace in pathos. It has the constancy of a flesh from which no hand can ever tear itself away.

Did Husserl ever anticipate what we are talking about? The following passage contains the aborted fate of phenomenology: "When something endures, then a passes over into xa', xa' into $yx'a''$, and so on. The production of consciousness, however, goes only from a to a'', from xa' to $x'a''$, and so on . . . the a, x, y, on the other hand, is nothing produced by consciousness. It is what is primally produced—the 'new,' that which has come into being alien to consciousness, that which has been received, as opposed to what has been produced through consciousness's own spontaneity" (ibid.).

Material phenomenology—a heading under which one can include the findings of *The Essence of Manifestation* along with my subsequent investigations—is not born from a reflection on the inadequacies of hyletic phenomenology and its ultimate failure. However, it may be the precondition for a clear perception of its inadequacies. It does not aim to complete what would have only been foreshadowed. What it puts into play in a radical way is the concept of matter, which became the "primary content," as it functions in its correlation with form, which became the intentional noesis. The pair impression/intentionality signifies that one sole and exclusive mode of manifestation and revelation has extended its reach over everything that is, namely, the mode expressed by intentionality. It casts aside everything that is non-intentional into the nonphenomenality of "content" or matter. Matter and Form belong to what the ek-stasis produces, as both its constituents and its results. This connection unites them throughout the history of Western metaphysics and is, in this respect, merely the result of its Greek origin.

"Matter," which material phenomenology understands in its clear opposition to the hyletic, no longer indicates the other of phenomenality but its essence. To the extent that in pure givenness it thematizes and explains its own self-givenness, material phenomenology is phenomenology in a radical sense. It no longer perceives objects, objects in their how, but an entirely new terrain in which there are no longer any objects. It is no longer governed by the laws of the world and thought, but by the laws of Life. Everything that the Greek phenomenon fails to clarify through its ek-static light, everything that the tradition did not know how to handle, what the modern philosophy of consciousness recovered in a crudely imagined unconscious that clings to it like the hump of a disguised character—this is what we truly are. This is what material phenomenology has the resources to recognize and aims to understand.

2

The Phenomenological Method

The question of method is so closely tied to phenomenology that phenomenology seems to be defined precisely by its specific method. The specificity of this method gives an indication of the concept of phenomenology, which appears first of all as a "methodological concept," according to Heidegger's explicit claim in *Being and Time*.[1] The present study aims for a systematic elucidation of the relation at work between method and phenomenology within the expression "phenomenological method." As to which of these is the guiding authority and as to the degree to which the concepts of method and phenomenology should be associated or dissociated, this is something that will only be able to be resolved at the end of our questioning.

This interrogation will take the five lectures given by Husserl in 1907 at the University of Göttingen as its guiding thread. One might imagine that this would be just a historical starting point marked with all of the precariousness and indeterminacy characteristic of every beginning. However, it is in these lectures that phenomenology returns to itself for the first time in order to understand itself in terms of its object and its means. It thus defines itself explicitly as a method, even though this is never anything more than a mode of access to an object and even though this mode of access must be defined on the basis of the object itself. The title of these 1907 lectures, "The Idea of Phenomenology," attests to the fact that phenomenology is aiming explicitly toward itself.

In this self-founding act, some decisions are made and some presuppositions are at work that are all the more visible because they are not covered over by the weight of later developments. In spite of its historical limitations, it is thus in this beginning that these decisions and presuppositions should be recognized. Phenomenology will never evade these presuppositions. Together they sketch out the finite circle of its future possibilities. First and foremost, it entails how phenomenology grasps itself as a method. This spontaneous understanding puts the method at the center of the problem, but in reality it remains the blind spot whose obscurity will evade almost all of the subsequent investigations. This thematization is explicit in appearance but never arrives at a true elucidation of the relation between phenomenology and its method, or more precisely, between the object of phenomenology and the mode of treatment that should be applied to it. What results is only their disastrous conflation. Yet, with respect to its grand obsession with a radical self-awareness, historical phenomenology has never been rivaled. The first attempt in 1907 puts before us a failure that will be continually repeated. Even today, phenomenology and philosophy are burdened by the weight of the enormous consequences of this failure.

The first lecture already arouses our concern. Phenomenology has always presented itself as introducing a rupture in the history of thought by means of a rejection of every tradition. It regards itself not as a historical beginning but as a more radical one, arising from itself and casting full light onto itself. Or, as this was already Descartes' ambition, it arises in the form of a recommencement. We see this claim to be compromised right away due to the relation introduced between phenomenology and the theory of knowledge in traditional philosophical thought. To be sure, this is not a natural thought, but a philosophical thought that is preoccupied with the possibility of knowledge. And as long as the possibility of knowledge is not established, no particular knowledge and notably no scientific knowledge can be established. For the project of founding knowledge moves in a circle, since each step of the foundation is a piece of knowledge that remains dubitable so long as the possibility of knowledge is not ensured.

Husserl escapes from this circle by a return to the Cartesian argument for doubt. Before the establishment of the possibility of knowledge, no piece of knowledge can be used. Everything is dubitable apart from the fact that I doubt. In the flood of false acts of cognition whose claims to truth are undone, there emerges a sphere of absolute and indubitable acts of cognition, namely, all of the *cogitationes*. For what is true about doubt is true about each one of them: each perception, representation, and judgment. Husserl claims, "However I might perceive, imagine, judge, infer ... it remains absolutely clear and certain that with respect to perception I am perceiving this or that, that with respect to judgment, I am judging this or that, etc." (Hua II 30/23–24).

This kind of claim is so laden with consequences that it determines the fate of phenomenology in a decisive manner. For that reason, it is important first to recall that it is not an isolated point; instead, it constitutes the leitmotif of the text, its touchstone, such that one finds numerous formulations of it. Let us cite the following instance: "Every intellectual experience, indeed every experience whatsoever, can be made into an object of pure seeing and apprehension while it is occurring. And in this act of seeing it is an absolute givenness. It is given as an existing entity, as a 'this-here.' It would make no sense at all to doubt its being" (Hua II 31/24).

In the two preceding quotations we observe from the outset a displacement that leads from the real *cogitatio*—from the real perception, the real representation, and the real judgment—to a regard directed toward them, which is a pure seeing in which one holds strictly to what is seen. For, it is under this regard, *in this pure gaze*, that the *cogitatio* becomes an absolute given.

The given and thus the absolutely given can be understood in two senses: as what is given, and as the character of being given, the fact of being given considered as such, more precisely, givenness or giving. The given ultimately depends on what gives. It is to the extent that giving is given truly, indubitably, and absolutely that the given is truly given. What is truly given is an absolute given whose being and existence are no longer contestable. The displacement of the real *cogitatio* by the pure regard directed toward it, the pure gaze by which it becomes an absolute given, unfolds the field of play in and through which the double meaning of *Gegebenheit* as the given and giving is fulfilled. The real *cogitatio* is the given, while the mode of the given—giving—is the pure gaze. It is an absolute giving because it posits nothing but what it truly sees, nothing but what it gives truly. And it is in this way that the given truly is, truly is seen, and exists.

The displacement of the real *cogitatio* by the pure gaze which gives it absolutely and in which it is an absolute given and the correlative duplication of the *Gegebenheit* in terms of the given and givenness put before us some errors, aporias, and absurdities of which it is important to become aware. The absurdity is that the real *cogitatio*, the one that should constitute the sphere of absolute knowing which the theory of knowledge needs simply in order to begin, is only an absolute given to the extent that it is submitted to a regard and a pure gaze. Consequently, it is only given to the degree to which, as a real *cogitatio*, it is subordinated to another power of givenness than itself. This other power gives it purely and absolutely, then and only then making it into an absolute given. The *cogitatio* is thus not an absolute given in and of itself but as the result of an external givenness that is added on to its own original being. Because the *cogitatio* is not in and of itself an absolute given, it can only become an absolute given in and through a pure gaze. The second text cited earlier says that "every intellectual experience [*vécu*], indeed every experience whatsoever, can be made into an object of pure seeing and apprehension *while it is occurring* [*pendant que nous le vivons*]. And in this act of seeing it is an absolute givenness" (ibid.).

The aporia that results from the displacement of the *cogitatio* by the pure gaze can be formulated in the form of two questions: (1) What, then, is the *cogitatio* before its arrival in the pure gaze and thus before becoming an absolute given? (2) What is this pure gaze and what can it possibly be besides a *cogitatio*? The *cogitatio* is thus a strange and capricious being. A first time, it does not bring about its own givenness and does not posit itself as an absolute given. But, a second time, it does this and thus becomes the absolute given that the phenomenology of knowledge needs. Let us admit that it is difficult to use the word essence with respect to the *cogitatio* when the concept of the *cogitatio* is still only a vague notion that covers over some key differences that these lectures and later phenomenology do not even perceive as questions.

If one examines the text more closely, the mystery only increases. The arrival of the *cogitatio* as an absolute given is not the sole fact pertaining to the pure gaze. This second *cogitatio* will confer the character that the first one does not have, namely, the absolute given. Recall the text, which says that "every experience whatsoever, can be made into an object of pure seeing and apprehension *while it is occurring*" (Hua II 31/24). It is not negligible for this to be cited in passing and thus presented as self-evident, without being questioned. It is to claim that the *cogito* must be realized actually each time that the regard of the pure gaze is directed toward it. Husserl notes: "While I am perceiving, I can also regard this perception in an act of pure seeing, just as it is" (Hua II 44/34). And again, "the being of the *cogitatio*, of experience as it occurs [*du vécu, pendant que nous le vivons*] and is simply being reflected on, cannot be doubted" (Hua II 4/62).

But if the *cogitatio* has already been carried out or if it is carried out while the regard takes it into its pure gaze, this is because the *cogitatio* is independent from and ontologically prior to the pure gaze. It is brought about or rather brings itself about independently. It is already there. The "there" of this already there is interpreted by the pure gaze as something there for itself, while at most it can only claim to see the *cogitatio*. The pure gaze can in no way claim its existence, which is presupposed as something already brought about or bringing itself about without it. Doubtless, the question that needs to be asked is how the *cogitatio* is brought about independently from the regard that tries to take it into its pure gaze. As a result of this question and its radical elaboration, the entire problem introduced in 1907 is struck at the heart and thrown into an aporia. Husserl, who believed himself to have escaped from the circle of knowledge in order to justify its possibility, has need of cognitions whose possibility has not yet been established. But this circle is not only methodological but also ontological. How can the existence of the *cogitatio* be founded starting from its being absolutely given in a pure gaze, if this pure gaze presupposes the prior existence of the *cogitatio*?

After the absurdity and the aporia, we now arrive at the error or rather the string of errors on the basis of which historical phenomenology constructs itself. Let us keep two of them in mind. The first is a historical one involving the return to Descartes. It has to do with the aberrant and universally rejected interpretation of the *cogito* as a piece of evidence and the first of all evidences. This would mean that the reality or the existence of the *cogitatio* would be founded on the pure gaze, on the *clara et distincta perceptio* that one can have of it. This evidence is produced through the mediation of a process of thought. At the end of this process, Descartes makes me see, such that I see on my own, that if I doubt and if I think, it is necessary that I exist, just as clearly as I see that "$2 + 3 = 5$." Unfortunately, the internal construction of the *cogitatio* is recognized due to the radical doubt that strikes down every evidence whatsoever and disqualifies this pure gaze about which Husserl speaks. Even if the gaze confines itself purely and firmly to what it sees, it cannot avoid error but rather is led into it, if seeing as such is fallacious. That is what Descartes supposes in the case of the *cogito*.

Besides, if the *cogitatio* were tributary in its reality to a regard and a pure gaze directed toward it and thus to a series of evidences entering into a thought process, it would need to be just as intermittent as these evidences themselves. It would depend on their realization, for the fulfilling or nonfulfilling of an intuition, whereas, for Descartes, the soul always thinks. This "always" indicates the autonomy of an essence that is irreducible to anything else and, in particular, to history as well as the vicissitudes of a gaze that is known to be dubious. One must say not only that the *cogitatio* is real independently from its givenness in a pure gaze, but also that *it is only on the condition of not being given in this way that it can be given.* In this way, we are led from Husserl's historical error to his fundamental philosophical error.

The critique of this philosophical error can be formulated in the following way: instead of being able to turn the *cogitatio* into an absolute given, the displacement of the *cogitatio* through its entry under the regard of thought causes it to disappear. It is not just a matter here of either a partial or provisional concealment. Even less is it a matter of a modification or alteration similar to what psychology describes such that, under the regard of attention, for example, mental processes are blurred to the point of occasionally breaking apart. It is an impossibility in principle: where the regard of thought, in its pure gaze, is concerned, the *cogitatio* does not stand. Instead of the regard being able to give the *cogitatio* as an absolute given that would reside in it and be identified with it, the regard de-realizes the *cogitatio* in an essential way. As for the *cogitatio*, the regard does not place it before us but only proposes the void to us. Has anyone ever seen his or her own thought, emotion, passion, or anxiety, unless he or she mistakes them for what is only an indication of them or what one interprets them to be? Our life is never and cannot be seen. Thus it could not be capable of being grasped in an evidence that is supposed to be absolutely given as it is in itself.

When Husserl speaks about the absolute givenness of the *cogitatio* in a pure gaze, he falls prey to a confusion. He confuses seeing and the seen; that which is totally seen in it, on one hand, and the *cogitatio*, on the other hand, which has nothing to do with the seen and belongs outside of its field. The proof of this confusion resides in the fact that it has already been carried out when, either in the phenomenological reduction or in the simple natural reflection, a gaze is directed toward the *cogitatio* in an attempt, albeit vain, to grasp it.

The first theoretical failure in the 1907 lectures is thus the displacement of the *cogitatio* in the pure gaze, which converts it into an absolute given, as if it were not already in and through itself, an original experience. Husserl sought this absolute givenness elsewhere, and by seeking it elsewhere, he will never be able to find it. As we have seen, this displacement implies a becoming, since it is only once it is brought into the evidence of the pure gaze that the *cogitatio* becomes the absolute givenness in question. By arbitrarily privileging a word from the Husserlian text, are we overestimating the condition under which the *cogitatio* must be submitted in order to be what it is in itself for Descartes? Or rather, should it not be recognized that this becoming determines the Husserlian problematic from beginning to end inasmuch as it is tantamount to the phenomenological method and primarily the phenomenological reduction? What motivates the reduction and what it prescribes is the need for a treatment that will lead the *cogitatio* to be changed into a pure phenomenon, a phenomenon in the phenomenological sense. Phenomenology will become possible on this basis. But must one not then ask, along with §7 of *Sein und Zeit* to which we will return: What needs to become a phenomenon for a mode of phenomenological treatment, if not "something which at first and most often does not show itself" or only does so in a confused and poorly understood way? (SZ 35/31).

We would not deny in any way that, as modes of thought, phenomenology, and philosophy in general are realized as this work of elaboration and elucidation in which scientific propositions are justified, in accordance with their own mode of temporality and their claim to be scientific. What we do contest from the outset is the mistake by which this trial of thought is taken for the trial of reality itself; the mistake by which the *cogitatio*'s coming into evidence under thought's gaze is taken for the essence of this *cogitatio*. Again, that is to say the mistake by which the reduced phenomenon, the pure phenomenon in the phenomenological sense, is taken to be the original essence of phenomenality as such and to be the essence of Life.

What does this "pure" and "reduced" phenomenon consist of? The reduction realizes the movement by which the *cogitatio* is placed under the regard of thought. In addition, it demands that this movement be restricted to what is actually seen in it, while everything that is not—whatever is only presumed or emptily intended—is set aside. It is clear that the reduction works on this basis and continually presupposes it. It does not presuppose this because there would be no reason for it to be completed, but because it is located in and only knows seeing. Its sole concern is to be truly one with the seen. That is to say, its concern is that everything that it sees is truly seen, seen absolutely by it, seen through and through, transparent as something totally seen, and a pure phenomenon pure in the sense of the coextensiveness of seeing and the seen. The reduction presupposes this because it never goes back on the hither side of itself and on the hither side of seeing. It is ultimately nothing but seeing. Thought is identified with this seeing and obeys only its internal teleology.

And what are the aim and the means of the entire method—the phenomenological method that takes the reduction as its point of departure and constantly relies on it—if not this giving something to be seen in and through seeing? And as for the possibility of knowledge that the phenomenology of knowledge aims to ensure, what does it consist of except for this seeing finally being perceived in its unique and exclusive role as a foundation, that is to say, as something below which it is not possible to return inasmuch as it is self-justified in the actuality of its act of seeing? As Husserl states in a foundational claim in the second lecture: "seeing cannot be demonstrated or deduced" (Hua II 38/30).

If, all the same, it is a matter of something other than blissfully contemplating everything that we see in immediate experience, and if, differing from natural knowledge in this way, the philosophical project wants to rely on the possibility of seeing as such, the establishment, or if you will, the recognition of this possibility is a phenomenological problem and, what is more, the problem which defines phenomenology in this 1907 approach. The response to this latter question is stunning: seeing must and actually does justify, by the act of seeing, the seeing that constitutes the possibility of knowledge and phenomenology itself. In order to found both phenomenology and knowledge—and to make phenomenology into a phenomenology of knowledge—it is necessary and sufficient therefore to bring this act of seeing into view, to "see this act of seeing itself" (Hua II 31/24).

The self-foundation of seeing will run throughout the doctrine. It will always consist of the intensification of seeing, as attested by the following proposition from a later text: "Only in seeing can I bring out what is truly present in a seeing; I must make a seeing explication of the proper essence of seeing."[2] This intensification marks the enclosure of seeing within itself, that is to say the unsurpassable and definitive assigning of phenomenality to seeing as such. In the introductory analyses of the 1907 lectures, the foundational power of seeing is not exercised immediately with respect to itself. This situation will be discovered only progressively, when the reality of the *cogitationes* will have been explicitly reduced to the reality of seeing. In their precarious but still presupposed autonomy, these *cogitationes* are offered to the gaze in the pure reflection of the reduction in order to become absolute givens. Husserl asked himself about the possibility of this type of reflection. It is not a seeing that itself gives what is seen. Following the requirements of the second lecture, the knowledge that is posited as presuppositionless sees what is offered to its potential gaze as already there and as already given.[3] The already given or the pregiven is the givenness of the retention, without which reflection would not be possible. The reflective regard would find nothing before itself. If it were not retained by retention, the *cogitatio* that it seeks to grasp would disappear when it turns back onto it. What, then, does the given of the retention as the pregiven for reflection consist of? It is a "seen," the already seen of a primal seeing; it is the retention itself.

According to the teachings of the lectures, we said that the *cogitatio* is only given in person as an absolute givenness at the end of a process of becoming, where it arrives under the gaze directed toward it and is changed into a pure phenomenon. Here the process of becoming that the *cogitatio* undergoes in order to arrive as a phenomenon can no longer be questioned. It is the process of becoming as such; it is time. It is the immediate sliding of the *cogitatio* into the past. This first dehiscence creates the separation in which the seen is able to arrive and to stand before the seeing. Henceforth, the seeing and the seen are possible. Only on the basis of and through this first separation of time is it possible for the *cogitatio* to arrive as a phenomenon in the gaze of seeing. A serious difficulty, it is true, is presented here. By becoming the absolute given of a pure phenomenon only in this way, the *cogitatio* or life would only exist in the past, according to a remark of Husserl's two years earlier. The absolute presence of absolute givenness is an absence. So, one must ask once again: What is the *cogitatio* in itself, prior to its coming into being or rather into the nothingness of the intentional ek-stasis? What is life as life, as the living present and not as no longer existing, as dead in the past?

When the process of thought in the phenomenological reduction and method is applied to the ek-static dehiscence of temporality, one can believe that it leads back to the process of being itself, if being is understood as time. This process of being, however, is adjusted to the process of thought and resembles it to the point of being one with it. What a convenience! What an appropriation! For Husserl already, the process of phenomenological clarification is hardly different from the temporal process of perception and is modeled on it—sequence by sequence, evidence for evidence. This punctual evidence vanishes at once into the flow, which carries it away. In the pure gaze of seeing, the *cogitatio* is not an absolute existence; instead, it falls off into the abyss of its disappearance; it is not being but rather nonbeing. This difficulty, which it runs up against from the outset, requires the burgeoning phenomenology to proceed without delay to completely redefine its themes as well as their mode of treatment. But let us allow Husserl to tell us all that himself.

The becoming/disappearance of the *cogitatio* in the pure gaze of seeing, first of all, entails the perversion of the categories with which the *cogitatio* must be thought in its reality, that is, the perversion of the fundamental concepts of phenomenology. The first of these is the concept of immanence. To be immanent signifies that the *cogitatio*, which is to say pure phenomenality in its original phenomenalization, becomes a phenomenon in itself without leaving itself and without producing any separation. Because the phenomenalization of the immanent givenness of the *cogitatio* is given without any separation, it gives nothing else, nothing that would be placed in the alterity of a distance. What it gives is itself, its own reality. The *cogitatio* thus gives its own reality to itself, inasmuch as it is immanence and exists through the work of immanence. Self-givenness (*Selbstgegebenheit*) exists only in the *cogitatio* and in the *cogitatio* alone. The pair givenness/given is only the expression of the way in which thought thinks everything that it thinks, precisely, in and through this duplication. But the self-givenness of the *cogitatio* implies that every duplication is abolished from its immanence.

Self (*Selbst*) in self-givenness thus signifies not only, as it does in the Husserlian text, that the thing given is given in itself, is shown in itself, in the nudity of its own reality, such as it appears and thus such as it is. This formal definition is appropriate for the perception of the wall in terms of its color, length, height, regularity or irregularity of its surface, possibly the materials out of which it is made, or where the paint has disappeared. In this givenness of the wall, there is the fact that the wall is different from its givenness. Its self, its *selbst*, is that of a thing or a being. But a thing by itself has no "self." When we say that the wall is shown "in itself," the "self" mentioned here is merely the external designation of the wall's identity with itself and its "individuality." This identity of the wall with itself, which individualizes it in contrast with every other and allows it to be shown as this wall, is itself an external identity. It is the wall in its exteriority with respect to itself, and in this way, in its identity with itself. But this wall, in its external identity with itself, is the phenomenon "wall" as an external phenomenon, as a phenomenon whose phenomenality is constituted by exteriority. The "self" of the wall, its identity with itself as its exteriority to itself, is an exteriority in which it is shown precisely in itself, as a "self," in its identity with itself. It is nothing but its givenness, to the extent that this givenness is constituted by exteriority, the phenomenality of the world, and the ek-stasis of Being.

When it comes to the *cogitatio*, self and thus self-givenness have an entirely different meaning. In the first place, the self is tied to givenness in an essential way. In this givenness of self (self-givenness), there is nothing else to consider henceforth but givenness itself, to the exclusion of every being and every thing. In the second place, givenness itself has changed. It no longer consists in the transcendent exteriority of a world but in an interiority so radical that every conceivable exteriority is banished from it. This interiority of self-givenness is the immanence of the *cogitatio*. In this immanence, the self of self-givenness does not refer exclusively to this. It happens that givenness and what is given are the same; it is a self-givenness in an original sense. In this sense, there is a self-givenness, a givenness of the self, in which givenness is given to itself as givenness and as giving. This original self-givenness of givenness is the self-experiencing of absolute subjectivity, that is to say subjectivity as such, the *cogitatio*.

The original ipseity is born in the self-experience of absolute subjectivity. It is the self grasped in its innermost possibility, to which every "self," even the most external one, secretly points back. If the wall has a "self" in such a way that it can be shown to us in itself and do so in its own exteriority to itself, this is only because this exteriority affects itself through the pathetic phenomenality of an auto-affection where there is no longer any exteriority and where the ipseity about which we are speaking reigns. It is only because the self-givenness of this ipseity belongs to every givenness whatsoever and, in particular, to the givenness of the wall, that the wall or any being whatsoever as a phenomenon can have, in and through this givenness alone, a "self." In addition to its givenness, the self of the being that enables it to be seen does not belong to it; it belongs to its givenness, ultimately to the self-givenness of the givenness whose essence is also the essence of every possible ipseity.

The important concept of *Selbstgegebenheit*, on which all being and every being must be built, thus refers to the fundamental category of phenomenology—immanence—and not to the mere banality of seeing. This immanence of the *cogitatio* is conceived by Descartes as an idea. This is why he writes, "By the word "idea" I understand all that which takes place in us that we of ourselves are immediately conscious of it."[4] The reality of the *cogitatio* as immanence is a reality of a very particular kind. It is the reality of appearing itself in its self-appearing. It is only because the *cogitatio* is immanent and because, ultimately conceived by Descartes as its own idea and as the form in which it immediately embraces itself, it is nothing other than the self-appearing of appearing, that it has and can have a reality of its own. By having this reality and experiencing itself, it is a self. It is only on the basis of this immanent essence of the *cogitatio*, which includes its ipseity within itself, that the concept of *Selbstgegebenheit* has and can have a sense.

In his "The Train of Thought in the Lectures," Husserl distinguishes between appearing and what appears. He contrasts them through an essential correlation in which the meaning of the concept of the "phenomenon" is twofold. What appears is the objectivity that figures into appearing, while the appearing is this figuration or appearing in consciousness. This contrast does not only make what appears differ from appearing, as an "objectivity" perceived within appearing. This objectivity can still overflow appearing itself. This is what happens, for example, when consciousness presumes to know something that is not truly given in it. In the *cogitatio*, to the contrary, what appears is not different from appearing and is identical to it as what results immediately from appearing. Thus appearing is defined in and through itself, in its self-appearing, as the phenomenological reality of this original phenomenality as such. Neither Husserl nor any subsequent phenomenology will ever care to elucidate the phenomenological reality of pure phenomenality. This is a task that we have assigned to material phenomenology and that defines it.

Yet, Husserl (and this is where he went further than all the other contemporary thinkers) never doubted that the *cogitatio* had its own reality, even if he left its appearing undetermined. This reality, which he calls *reell*, causes the ontological weight of being to tip into absolute subjectivity and it alone. Impression and intentionality, whose relationship was already examined in the preceding study, belong as the essential components of the reality of the *cogitatio* and are also called real.

The 1907 lectures contrast this radical concept of immanence of which they are not unaware with a second concept of immanence. The essence of this latter concept reveals itself to be structurally heterogeneous to the immanence of the *cogitatio* and can be understood only by putting the *cogitatio* out of play. In order to rise to this second concept of "immanence," one should position oneself in seeing and practice the reduction within it, restricting oneself to what is really seen in and through seeing. What is it that is really seen in the pure gaze of the reduced seeing? The *cogitatio*. But, then, it is clear that the real *cogitatio*—as it experiences itself in the immanence of its self-appearing—is no longer in question. It is the *cogitatio* submitted to a phenomenological mode of treatment and to the reduced seeing. Here the *cogitatio* is no longer a real moment of subjectivity, instead it is an object of knowledge toward which the regard of thought goes beyond itself in order to grasp it in its pure seeing. Thought's grasp of a content situated outside of itself, and in this way, seen by it, is a transcendence in the first sense that Husserl recognizes in this concept. Transcendence thus understood is equivalent to immanence in the second sense, which is the immanence of *cogitatio*'s pure seeing. Once immanence receives the meaning of transcendence, the perversion of the fundamental concepts of phenomenology is complete.

Why is the transcendent grasp of the *cogitatio* still called immanence? Because when seeing is limited strictly to the grasp of what is seen, what is seen becomes completely contained in seeing, fully perceived in it, and consequently "immanent" to this regard. This kind of immanence, whose main possibility resides in the transcendence of seeing, is in Husserl's eyes what defines "absolute and clear givenness, self-givenness in the absolute sense [*absolute und klare Gegebenheit, Selbstgegebenheit im absoluten Sinn*]" (Hua II 35/27).

At the same time as the perversion of the concept of immanence has led it to signify its contrary, it has insurmountably excluded from itself the fulfillment of an "absolute givenness" and "self-givenness in an absolute sense." For in the transcendence of seeing, it has been shown that the *cogitatio* is in fact never present "in person" and in its reality. This presence of the *cogitatio* can only be experienced in itself, in its immanence. In order to justify the application of the concept of immanence to the gaze of the *cogitatio*—that is, to transcendence—Husserl invents a second concept of transcendence, which refers to the case in which knowledge, by intending or positing an object, does not see itself and in which the aim is thereby no longer actually contained in what is seen. With this transcendence in the second sense, Husserl says, "we go beyond what is given in the genuine sense, beyond what can be directly seen and apprehended" (Hua II 35/28).

The first transcendence is a departure from the reality of the *cogitatio*. The second transcendence is a departure from the seen of seeing. But the second transcendence presupposes the first one. To surpass the seen of seeing toward the intended or the presumed can be possible only on the basis of a first aim that has already brought about the departure from the reality of the *cogitatio*. It is in one single ontological setting that seeing actualizes itself, whether it limits itself to what it sees or whether it surpasses what it sees toward the presumed. The difference between the first and second concepts of transcendence is a secondary difference. Insofar as this transcendence is thrown toward a horizon opening beyond what is seen and in which what is seen refers to a not yet seen or an already seen, one must even ask whether this difference can be maintained, because what is seen is a mere punctual presence and an ideal limit of the flow, which is not yet something already seen and will change into something out of sight, the unseen, the "unconscious" into which everything belonging to the world fades.

At any rate, what is "completely present to the gaze" in the "immanence" of the first transcendence of seeing aimed toward the *cogitatio* has nothing in common with the presence of the *cogitatio* in its immanence. This latter immanence carries neither a horizon nor a world within itself. It has nothing that would be capable of being seen and of changing into an unseen or vice versa. It differs from the first transcendence so completely that, while the first immanence remains like an unshakeable presence and the absolute givenness of the absolute presence of our life itself, the complete presence of what is immanent to the regard is only a complete absence of the *cogitatio*. In this way, Husserl's attempt to give a positive sense to the immanence of the *cogitatio* in the pure gaze of seeing and to the evidence resulting from the phenomenological reduction and method is seriously weakened. It is even totally reversed, if one notes that the impossibility of the *cogitatio* to come into the sight of seeing is not the impossibility of transcendent being, which is in principle constituted in and through this type of grasp.

An ontological threat weighs on the immanent contents of seeing, that is to say, on the *cogitationes*, which have become givens for the pure gaze in the reduction. Unconsciously, Husserl attempts to avert this threat by quickly surmounting the essential difference that was just drawn between the two concepts of immanence and by taking it to be negligible. Thus, the stupefying statement: "(the) *cogitationes* present a sphere of absolute immanent givenness, whatever else we may mean by immanence" (Hua II 43/33). It is as if the givens could be independent from the mode of their givenness and indifferent to the radical and more original difference that splits their modes of givenness, that is, indifferent to the phenomenalization of phenomenality as such! It as if the immanent given could be absolute in the same sense, whether they belong to the innermost reality of the *cogitatio* or whether they are instead cast outside of it as the transcendent content of an ek-static seeing. The passage immediately following this statement refers explicitly to this second givenness in which immanence means the transcendence of seeing in evidence. The absolute character of the immanent given, which it receives from the first givenness of the *cogitatio*, is henceforth related to and founded on the second one alone. It is founded on the gaze of seeing. Husserl explains: "In the seeing of the pure phenomenon the object is not external to knowledge, or to 'consciousness'; rather, it is given in the sense of the absolute self-givenness of what is simply seen" (ibid.). A mutation of phenomenology's conception of phenomenality takes place here, and it affects the founding of phenomenology. Here the absolute meaning of givenness and thus of the given is transferred from the immanence of the *cogitatio* to the transcendence of a pure gaze and is supposed to be unchanged by this transfer. Without any other form of trial, the latter takes the place of the former and hides it for good.

Immanence having been reduced to transcendence and the original phenomenological question of the reality of the *cogitatio* already lost, phenomenology goes in a direction that prescribes the mode of givenness to which it is limited. This paradoxical limitation of a problem that, in its "Cartesian path," is defined on the basis of the *cogitatio* but, from its very first steps, separates itself from the true reality of the *cogitatio*, can be explained by the obscurity in which this original reality of the *cogitatio* is shrouded by its nature and thus by the difficulty of understanding it. The same difficulty gives rise to the sliding from the first concept of immanence to the second and thereafter the unilateral thematization of immanence.

Another fact, however, should not escape us: by only thematizing the mode of givenness of the transcendence of a pure gaze and by doing so under the false title of "immanence," phenomenology retains but one domain of being—one that suits it perfectly. The phenomenological work of clarification has every liberty to exert itself and to be pursued there. It is a domain of being offered to the seeing of thought and conceived on the basis of thought. It offers a being for thought, to be thought, that is to say, seen—seen in every sense, in all the various dimensions and ways that it can be seen. The phenomenological reduction and method are the first signs that thought is posited in this world in order to prepare and to allow an exhaustive delineation of the world. That is why henceforth phenomenological thought will rely absolutely on this world that seeing has opened to it.

The third lecture repeats all of the propositions according to which what is seen is being and absolutely what is. It is simply a matter of making it the case that what is seen is truly seen. The reduction's rejection of transcendence in the second sense aims only to expand the reign of the first transcendence, which is the reign of seeing. What must be set aside as "transcendent" is only what is not seen, what transcendence does not reach. Everything that exists is only for transcendence and must be capable of being actually reached by it. Husserl states, "Only through a reduction . . . do I acquire an absolute givenness that no longer offers anything transcendent" (Hua II 44/34). This must be understood in the second sense of transcendence. What can be recognized in many ways is that this elimination of transcendence in the second sense signifies nothing but the liberation of transcendence pure and simple and thus of the world as such.

Transcendence in the second sense acts so as to refer mental processes to a psychological ego situated in the empirical world. In this way, the most common perception we have of ourselves is a natural apperception. To eliminate or to suspend transcendence in the second sense is to regain this mental process, which is reduced to itself. It is reduced to the pure gaze of the phenomenological reflection and thus, as Husserl explains, is a pure phenomenon:

> If I place the ego and the world and the experience of the ego as such in question, then reflection upon what is given in the apperception of the relevant experience . . . yields the phenomenon of this

apperception: the phenomenon, roughly, of "perception apprehended as my perception" ... The perception thus grasped and delimited in "seeing" is then an absolute perception, devoid of every transcendence, given as a pure phenomenon in the phenomenological sense. (Hua II 44/34)

With this suspension of positing a non-immanent being, for example, the suspension of the empirical ego situated in its temporal world, phenomenology is separated from psychology. It takes possession of its "objects," these pure phenomena taken "as entities absolutely given and grasped in pure immanent seeing" (Hua II 45/34). Phenomenology is rightly a "science of pure phenomena" (Hua II 46/35).

The elimination of the second transcendence in the phenomenological reduction, as it is presented in these lectures, which is to say from its beginning, reveals for us the narrowness of its scope. For, in this *epoche* of the world, only the empirical world and the psychological ego inscribed in it, only the contents of this world and the belief in them, are suspended. The *epoche* does not suspend the world itself—the horizon of visibility where everything that can be seen is shown—this place of light in which evidence is put forward as presence in order to concentrate all its luminosity within it. This is indeed the sense or the reversal of sense of this passage from one transcendence—the one that is excluded—to the other one which is exalted by this exclusion: the elevation of pure transcendence to the rank of a universal ontological category and to the condition of everything that is.

Here the great turning point of these 1907 lectures appears. At the very moment when, in abandoning true immanence, phenomenology proceeds to this celebration of seeing, there emerges in it the strange process by which, first secretly and then explicitly, it renounces its most ultimate claim, namely, the ontological claim to give being. Phenomenology does not carry out this ultimate sacrifice, the sacrifice of reality and life, in the redoubled seeing of absolute self-consciousness; instead, it carries this out in another way, an indirect way, which determines it altogether. Its theme shifts—analyses that were not a part of the program suddenly unfold their implications with the sole aim of allowing access to new objects that substitute for the lost reality. Phenomenology allows its mourning, which it harbors without yet fully knowing it, to be recognized through this complete reordering of its objectives along with the many other signs which are indications of it.

Husserl's genius is certainly to have anticipated that this reordering and the thematic turn it implies would be necessary and to have set forth the conditions for it from the outset, in such a way as to make it possible and unnoticed. In his interpretation of the *cogito* he is completely wrong (though he is not alone in this), but he has already paid the price for this error. The existence of the *cogitatio*, on his view, is established insofar as, by entering into the gaze of phenomenological reflection's seeing and thus in the evidence of this pure gaze, it has become an absolute given and thus indubitable. Husserl observes, "The 'existence' of the *cogitatio* is guaranteed by its absolute self-givenness, by its givenness in pure evidence" (Hua II 8/65). But if, instead, this existence or reality of the *cogitatio* slips away in principle from the regard of phenomenological reflection and thus from the "pure evidence" of its seeing, and if, as we have already established, it is never an absolute personal-presence in the Husserlian sense, it is striking to realize that this ontological collapse is announced and in some way accepted from the start of the text and, in particular, in an extraordinary parenthesis in the third lecture, whose testimony we can now gather: "Descartes asked, as you will recall, after he had established the evidence of the *cogitatio* (or rather, in a phrase we have not adopted, the *cogito ergo sum*)" (Hua II 49). Thus, at the very moment when he commits his most serious error of reducing the *cogitatio* to the evidence that gives it, Husserl confusedly recognizes that one must choose between the evidence of the *cogitatio* and its existence. Descartes founded the existence of the *cogitatio* on itself, on its internal phenomenological structure as the form of the immediate perception through which the *cogitatio* is aware of itself, consequently without any mediation and without the mediation of evidence, in particular, which is believed to be dubitable in this case. This is what Husserl cannot imagine, insofar as he reduces the most perfect formulation of givenness to evidence. The entire problem involves this reduction, which is the phenomenological reduction itself. But this is to forget that for Descartes the foundation of knowledge in the *clara et distincta perceptio* is introduced only at the beginning of the third meditation, after the *cogito* has been established. The *cogitatio* is thus entirely independent from the dubitable evidence of cognition, even though Husserl seeks to submit it to evidence. Along with this mistake, however, comes the confused but important intuition that, inasmuch as one wants to offer the *cogitatio* to the gaze of seeing, the reality or existence of the *cogitatio* is lost.

How can one not be surprised by the strange fate of the *cogitatio* once it is submitted to the reduction? This uncontested existence, which is held completely in seeing and is kept by the power of its vision and its will as long as it wants, is adrift. It is carried away by a sliding that has always already begun without any present that might have truly preceded it and without any reality ever unfolding its essence in a present that would be the presence of real being and thus this real being itself. The reduction ought to provide a pure field of existence founded on and identical to this pure presence. We see this field fall apart right before our eyes. Faced with this dislocation or rather this disappearance, we are forced to recognize that there has never been anything concerning the existence and reality of the *cogitatio* that we could have seen. Husserl observes, "We move in the field of pure phenomena. But why do I say 'field'—is it not rather an eternal Heraclitean stream of phenomena?" (Hua II 47/36).[5]

These pure phenomena brought by the reduction, however, should have offered us with absolute givens that knowledge needs in order to escape from the circle of its self-foundation. But what pieces of knowledge and what judgments can be based on evanescent givens that are never truly present? How would they be able to provide adequate support for propositions aiming to be scientific, which is to say apodictic and universal? Right after recognizing the condensation of the field of pure phenomena into a Heraclitean stream, Husserl adds, "What statements can I make about it? While I am seeing it, I can say: this here!—it exists, indubitably. . . . But obviously there is nothing by way of 'objective' validity about these statements. They have no 'objective sense'" (Hua II 47/36). And again: "Thus we will not attribute any particular value to such judgments as 'This is here' and the like, which we make on the basis of pure seeing" (Hua II 48/36). And then: "Phenomenological judgments, as particular judgments, are not terribly instructive" (ibid.).

Yet, the rationality to be constructed on the basis of these precarious givens is not the only thing that vacillates. This theoretical weakening is only the effect of an ontological weakening affecting the givens themselves. This ontological weakening means that the existence that should be posited in and with such givens is in fact not capable of being posited. For, it is precisely on his own ground, in analyzing what is entirely seen in the seeing of the reduction, that Husserl himself will draw up the report about the nonexistence of the *cogitatio* in the absolute phenomenon that should have demonstrated it beyond any possible doubt.

This report is not pleasant. So, we see in a paradoxical way that at the moment of the ontological foundation of absolute subjectivity, which is in spite of everything the *cogito*, Husserl works to devalue the relation of the concept of existence to the *cogitatio*, that is to say, he devalues what it has to do with reality. The *cogitatio* is not an existence worthy of the name. It is not a true existence capable of founding rationality, because it is "singular." What does this epithet, which, in the rest of these lectures, will be attached in a pejorative way to the *cogitationes*—so as to disqualify them and ultimately to justify *their elimination from the problem*—mean? It marks the irreducibly limited character of a fragment of a mental process. As a this-here (*Dies-da*), the singular is destined, in its ephemeral occurrence, to slide into nonbeing. Here the concept of singularity is the equivalent of individuality, which is to understand it in terms of the *principium individuationis* that defines the individuality or the singularity of a thing by its place in time. When, after the reduction, time has become immanent phenomenological time (in the second sense of the immanent), the "singular" *cogitationes* are the *cogitationes* perceived in phenomenological time. They are ek-statically projected in time according to the current future, now and past; they are moving appearances, through which "objects" are intended but not intended in themselves. They are ungraspable profiles taken up into the flux and flowing away with it.

Here the concept of singularity is taken outside of its place of origin, where it refers to nothing but the internal structure of the *cogitatio* according to the idea of an ipseity that marks it with its transcendental stamp. This ipseity affects itself as the self it is and through which all of its various modalities are those of this self. They are the *cogitationes* of an Ego. So, by abandoning the givenness of the real *cogitatio*, the reduction would likewise lose all of its properties, for example, its transcendental particularity. It would regain the *cogitatio* only as an unexplained nature, where it is nothing more than the seen of a seeing, more precisely, an immanent given in the internal consciousness of time.

But then, all of the categories and presuppositions of phenomenology are shaken at their roots. The concept of singularity loses sense by designating the individuation of the temporal mental process by its place in phenomenological time, in place of its radical ipseity as the idea of the original *cogitatio*. This loss of sense results from the substitution of the "immanence" of the mental process self-constituted in ek-static temporality for the original immanence of the *cogitatio*. Truly speaking, that is what the phenomenological reduction is: *it is the passage from immanence in the first sense to immanence in the second sense*. It is the entry of the real *cogitatio* into the seeing of phenomenological reflection and thus into the flow. But this entry of the *cogitatio* into the pure gaze that would seek to turn it into absolute givenness in person produces the opposite effect. What should have been completely seen and contained in the pure gaze, the "immanent" in the reassuring sense of what is entirely there under the regard, overflows the regard in every direction. In this act of surpassing, it becomes its contrary—the transcendent. This should not surprise us, however, if it is true that immanence in the second sense—the given of phenomenological time—is in fact transcendent in the first sense, that toward which consciousness goes beyond itself in the self-objectification of its self-temporalization, and if the transcendent in the first sense is necessarily also the transcendent in the second sense, insofar as in the process of this ek-static self-temporalizing, everything overflows the horizon of the present from every side and casts it outside of itself throughout the depths of its being.

Husserl recognized this breakup of the "immanent" given in the reduction—a given that took the place of the *cogitatio*—once he pushed the analysis further and thought the condition of the reduction and reflection in terms of retention. From this moment on, absolute givenness had its essence in the flow in which there is no longer any remnant of what is not flowing; there is no longer any absolute givenness, but only a disappearing at each instant. "So," says the fifth lecture, "we seem to have fallen into a pretty kettle of fish" (Hua II 70/52). The cause of this problem, as the text immediately indicates, is the mistake on which all phenomenology is constructed and by which the *cogitatio* is reduced to the evidence that one is supposed to have of it: "We began with the evidence of the *cogitatio*" (ibid.). Having made this error, the consequences are as follows:

> At first, it appeared that we were on firm ground—*being pure and simple*. One had simply to grasp it and to see it. . . . It now turns out that the pure being of the *cogitatio* does not present itself as so simple a matter; it turns out that diverse forms of objectivity "constitute" themselves in the Cartesian sphere, and that "constitution" means that things given immanently are not, as it first appeared, in consciousness as things are in a box, but rather that they present themselves in something like "appearances" . . . appearances that in a certain sense create objects for the ego in their changing and highly peculiar structure. (Hua II 71/52)

The synopsis of the fifth lecture is even more explicit: "Things are a bit less accommodating, however, once we consider what is given more closely. First: the *cogitationes*, which we consider to be simply given and therefore entirely unmysterious, conceal all sorts of transcendences" (Hua II 11/67). The cause of the breaking apart of the simply given—the pure being which it would suffice to look at—is clearly indicated here. Transcendence gnaws away at this supposed presence of an "immanent" given within phenomenological time and makes it so that this presence is not immanent. On one hand, these immanent phenomenological appearances are the bearers of rays through which objects are constituted, while on the other hand, the appearances are themselves constituted in phenomenological time. They are transcendences at the heart of the primordial transcendence of temporality. In this way, they are given over to the laws that rule every transcendence: the laws of the finitude of the ek-static horizon in which what is given to us is placed before us as something "transcendent" and the laws of the disappearing resulting directly from the finitude of this pure place whereby appearances are only given one after another, in the negating stream of the flow. As a result, the *cogitatio* reduced to this immanent given is nothing but evanescent.

Now that the cause of the ontological collapse in which reality was lost has been elucidated in terms of the mode of treatment that was believed to be needed by and applicable to the *cogitatio* and to phenomenality itself, the result of this ontological collapse stands right before us: it is what we are calling the thematic turn. It consists of phenomenology's explicit and deliberate decision to give itself new objects in place of the *cogitatio* that escapes it: "The particular phenomenon of knowledge, coming and going in the stream of consciousness, is not the object of phenomenological determination" (Hua II 55/41). In this statement, there are two reasons motivating this change of theme. They both refer to the precariousness of the former object: the *cogitatio*. The first is that the givenness of the *cogitatio*, its appearing, instead of being the sought after absolute, cannot be dissociated from its own, immediate disappearance, to the point that appearing and disappearing are one in the flow. They are the flow and the streaming as such. This profound reason for the thematic displacement is overdetermined and very quickly covered over by another one, which has to do with the attempt of phenomenology and thus philosophy, as a phenomenological philosophy, to be scientific. Scientific propositions, as we have shown, can only be founded on true givens that are particular *cogitationes*. In their presence one can indeed say, "this, here, now, in this way." But one cannot in any way ensure that it will be the same later, for this is what will not appear. The *cogitationes* are like the clouds of the sky. It is impossible to establish universal propositions on givens like these. Even this very proposition that we just formulated would be impossible if it did not aim, through facticity and beneath it, toward what is from another order: its essence, that is, a group of necessary properties that the universal propositions only express. The affirmation on which phenomenology is founded is not "this is given" but "the givenness of any reduced phenomenon is an absolute and indubitable givenness" (Hua II 50/38). This affirmation is precisely not a particular proposition, a particular judgment, which has nothing to teach us; instead, it is a general proposition intending the essence and resting on it. This is the key thematic shift by which phenomenology is presented as "a rigorous science," the substitution for the simple, actual givens of particular *cogitationes* with their essence.

In spite of its legitimacy and perhaps its necessity, now one must see why this rational motivation for the thematic turn still only constitutes its apparent meaning, hiding the other meaning that, in and through the turn, phenomenology has lost. It is impossible to hide our surprise: Taking into view the essence of the *cogitatio*, this kernel of intelligibility and being is what makes each *cogitatio* be what it is each time and determines all of its characteristics. In this way, it introduces an apodictic discourse capable of stating these characteristics *a priori*. Would this be anything less than the mere acknowledgement of the chance appearing and certain disappearance of these characteristics? How can this paradox be maintained any longer?

This can be maintained by simply recalling the object of phenomenology. The object of phenomenology is not the things but their how. Prior to the thematic shift, things are *cogitationes*; afterward, they are their essences. As long as one is situated on the level of things, the displacement leading from the *cogitationes* considered in their particular and changing properties to the essence that prescribes these properties to them constitutes an undeniable thematic enrichment. It allows one to go beyond facticity and toward the *a priori* that rules it. But if one sets aside the level of things and enters into phenomenology's own problematic, one comes to question the mode by which these things are given. Then, the thematic shift changes its direction and, truly speaking, is totally reversed. How are the *cogitationes* given to us in their "factual existence," in what they comprise of the real, in their reality? This burgeoning phenomenology knows nothing about this. Or rather, to this crucial question in which everything is and must be decided, it immediately brings a spurious reply which it believes to be borrowed from Descartes: the *clara et distincta perceptio*.

And now without any transition let us raise the second question: How is the essence of the *cogitatio*—and no longer the *cogitatio* itself—given to us? It is given as the object of the intentional regard whose seeing is directed toward it to grasp it as its seen, as a transcendent object. By substituting for the mere acknowledgment of the existence of particular *cogitationes* and the particular judgments that one can make of them with the grasping of their essence, the 1907 thematic turn attempts to introduce us to the sphere of scientific and theoretical apodicticity, but it has done something completely different. It has substituted the mode of givenness of immanence whose original making, as the reality of the *cogitatio*, it proves unable to know with the sole mode of givenness that it does know, with the givenness of this transcendence and the seeing that founds it. The displacement at work here does not primarily concern objects or "what appears"; it concerns appearing itself. It is a phenomenological displacement in the radical sense, calling phenomenality itself into question. By setting aside the domain of facts, it abandons the original how of phenomenality.

This link between the thematic displacement and the properly phenomenological question of phenomenality as such can be seen to completely determine the Husserlian text. Phenomenology can in its concern for rationality—or because life just escaped from it—forget its fundamental presuppositions, indeed, the phenomenological requirement. Its work is carried out entirely within the reduction and its results only have validity, in its eyes, but it does so at this price. The essence cannot escape these conditions; it can be introduced into the investigation and take the place of the weakened *cogitatio* only as a "pure phenomenon" and as the absolute given of a pure gaze. But can it do this? It is remarkable that the entire problem that follows the thematic turn is governed by this question and tries to face up to it.

If the phenomenological reduction is the reduction to pure seeing and absolute givenness as the givenness in this seeing, the question is then about the extension of pure seeing and thus of absolute givenness: how far does this extend—to the field of everything that is or can be taken into the vision of seeing? Is essence, whether it involves the *cogitatio* or any essence whatsoever, included in or capable of being included in this field?

Inasmuch as it is tied to the thematic turn and emerges from it nearly inevitably, the question about the extension of pure seeing and the absolutely given is not posed in an indeterminate way; it refers concretely to a starting point. Extension is understood only relative to a prior limitation. What limitation is involved here? It is the limitation through which the question of pure seeing is initially posed in strict union with the question of the *cogitatio*, pure seeing being what turns the *cogitatio* into a phenomenon. We have examined the crucial implications of this situation, including the fact that, when the power of manifestation is entrusted to pure seeing, from the outset the *cogitatio* is deprived of this power and instead submitted to pure seeing. The initial relation between pure seeing and the *cogitatio* is precisely not an original relation, a relation of unity, as if they each referred to the same thing. Quite the contrary, a radical dissociation is at work between them that cannot be surmounted. The dissociation between givenness and the given is such that givenness pertains to seeing alone, while the *cogitatio* is lowered to the rank of the given.

For, after having secretly provoked the thematic turn, this prior dissociation determines the entire problem that flows from the thematic turn. The extension of pure seeing means its extension beyond the sphere of *cogitationes*. This can happen only because the link between the pure gaze and the *cogitatio* solely has a historical significance, one that is internal to the unfolding of the phenomenological problem and the reduction. It is not an essential link, because pure seeing and the *cogitatio* are and can be separated. They are separated in the way described above: pure seeing refers to the appearing and is identical to it, while the *cogitatio* is in fact only a "given," "what appears" in and through this appearing. But then it becomes clear that appearing "extends" beyond any particular "what appears," taking in its sight everything that it does illuminate and is capable of illuminating. Unlike the *cogitatio*, pure seeing thus does not have to be limited to a particular given; it founds and is coextensive with every conceivable given of every order whatsoever. In this way, the *cogitatio* is no more than an example through which pure seeing proves the excellence of its power. The *cogitatio* is only an absolute given insofar as it is seen, well seen, and thereby indubitable. Husserl states, "With Descartes we can now take the additional step (*mutatis mutandis*): whatever is given through *clear and distinct perception, as it is in any particular* cogitatio, we are entitled to accept" (Hua II 49/37).

Once the liberation of pure seeing from the *cogitatio* and its absolutization as a first and absolute givenness justified in and by itself are established, its link with the *cogitatio* becomes contingent. The *cogitatio* was only a particular example that provided an opportunity for thought to recognize the absolute power of seeing as it attains and reveals being in its seeing. The question about the extension of pure seeing, which is raised quite naturally, is thus found to be resolved already. Why should pure seeing be arbitrarily limited to the *cogitatio*, since the faculty of producing absolute knowledge and pure phenomena resides in pure seeing and in no way in the *cogitatio* that can become a pure phenomenon, an absolute knowledge, only through pure seeing? Instead of being tributary to a particular or privileged object on the basis of which one would attempt to circumscribe its domain of application, pure seeing is deployed on its own basis, in a perfect autonomy. The question of its extension is resolved by the strength of its seeing: wherever there can and will be a pure seeing, there will also be a pure phenomenon, an absolute givenness, an absolute knowledge. This potentially immense field is the field of phenomenology.

In this field, however, one object in particular holds our attention; it is precisely the one that has replaced the *cogitatio* as a theme and essence of the analysis, namely, the universal. It is what motivated the question about the extension of pure seeing, wanting to receive its own legitimacy from pure seeing. For if the universal essence can replace the *cogitatio* in an approach that is strictly limited to the reduction and seeks to be based on pure phenomena alone, this can take place on the condition of giving itself as a pure phenomenon. The question is thus no longer only to ask, in some sort of indeterminate way, how far seeing extends: "If we hold onto the self-givenness which, as we have already established, is not the self-givenness of real [*reeller*] particulars, say, the absolute particulars of the *cogitatio*, then the question arises as to how far this self-givenness extends and to what extent, or in what sense, it is bound to the sphere of the *cogitationes* and the generalizing universals drawn from the sphere" (Hua II 61/46).[6] It is rather a matter of carrying out the opposite movement, and by starting from the universal, to question the possibility for it to enter into pure seeing and to become a pure phenomenon and an absolute given like, for example, the particular *cogitatio*.

Indeed, Husserl took care to write in the second lecture, when the *cogitationes* were presented still as privileged objects of seeing and thus as absolutely given, "We see them, and, as we are seeing them, we can examine their essence, their constitution, their immanent character and conform our talk by a pure measure to what is seen in the fullness of its clarity" (Hua II 31/25). But the problem is really the possibility for the sense of the *cogitatio* to be examined in pure seeing. After the thematic shift, the fourth lecture asks, "But can universality, can general essences, and the general states of affairs that belong to them, actually achieve the same kind of self-givenness that a *cogitatio* does?" (Hua II 56/41).

Husserl's response is extraordinary, since it draws a strict dividing line between what belongs to the reality of the *cogitatio* as true immanence and what is situated outside of it and is thus transcendent. Husserl will take sides explicitly and deliberately in favor of the transcendent, rejecting the contrary attitude as a prejudice that one naively believes to be phenomenology as the philosophy of absolute subjectivity. What belongs to the reality of the *cogitatio* is the consciousness or the knowledge of the universal. After the reduction, it will appear as an "absolute phenomenon," as a "given." But, the text goes on to say, "we will search in vain for the universal that is supposed to be identical in the strongest sense across like immanent contents of innumerable possible acts of knowing" (ibid.). The universal, as the identity of many different thoughts, is necessarily transcendent to each one of them. Husserl elaborates: "Each real [*reelle*] part of the phenomenon of knowing, of this phenomenological particularity, is itself a particularity. Thus the universal, which is not a particularity, cannot be really contained in the consciousness of universality" (Hua II 56/42). Then there follows this surprising assertion: "But one could take exception to this kind of transcendence only on the basis of a prejudice" (ibid.).

How can transcendence cease to be problematic in a philosophy that uses the phenomenological reduction and puts transcendence out of play precisely because it is problematic? The text refers to "this" transcendence. But, what sort of transcendence is not problematic? The answer: the one that is in pure seeing. Pure seeing is substituted for the *cogitatio* and thereafter takes on the work of givenness in its stead. This is what the subsequent passage attests to with a striking clarity: "One must get especially clear on the fact that the absolute phenomenon, the reduced *cogitatio*, does not count as an absolute givenness because it is a particular, but rather because it displays itself in pure seeing after the phenomenological reduction as something that is absolutely self-given. But in pure seeing we can discover that universality is no less such an absolute givenness" (Hua II 56/42).

And in fact, to the degree that the sight of pure seeing is the original transcendence, what other type of being than transcendent being and the intentional object would be more able to give itself to this transcendence and to be the seen of this seeing? This would certainly not be the reality of the *cogitatio*, which is unable in its radical immanence to ever become the object of any seeing! Quite the opposite, the transcendent being is being-seen. The extension of the pure seeing of particular *cogitationes* to their universal essences is not an "extension" in the proper sense of the term. Instead, it conveys a radical discontinuity. It is the rupture between two domains that are forever separated: that of the universal and the transcendent being, on one hand, for which pure seeing is shown to be the adequate mode of access, and, on the other hand, its domain of incompetence, the *cogitatio*. Thus the abandonment of the particular for the universal does not signify a thematic displacement of the object, but as we have shown, it is a phenomenological displacement in the radical sense. It is the displacement of the ungrasped givenness of the *cogitatio* by transcendence and the givenness that suits it: the transcendent given and, in particular, the universal essence.

Once the possibility for the universal to be given in a pure seeing as much as the *cogitatio*—and truly a lot better than it—is established in principle, it suffices to establish it de facto in evidence. Husserl attempts to do this with the universal term "red," which appears as something seen in itself and given in person, if it is taken in the attitude of reduction and gives up all of its transcendent meaning. One no longer considers it as the red of this ink blotter or of any other object but as a pure red, as a universal that is what it is independently from the object from which seeing has pulled it. Redness thus becomes a purely "immanent" given, which is truly grasped in itself through a pure seeing and does not exceed this seeing in any way. Husserl never expressed more clearly that the immanent is the transcendent pure and simple, something that the regard goes out toward and attains directly. In contrast with this true immanence, one must now distinguish a false immanence, namely, the *cogitatio* itself! Husserl concludes: "Thus, this givenness (of the red) is a purely immanent givenness, *not immanent in the false sense, namely, existing in the sphere of individual consciousness*" (Hua II 57/42).

The thought of the universal allows us to prove two points. First, it shows that the extension of pure seeing and its correlate, absolute givenness, reaches beyond the sphere of the *cogitationes*. For the universal is precisely not a *cogitatio*; it stands beyond the plurality of consciousnesses that are directed toward it. In this beyond, it shows itself to them as the sole transcendent term of their multiple aims. In this transcendence, which is external to them, they see the universal, in and of itself, as a pure givenness. By entering into pure seeing, the general extends the domain of pure seeing; at the same time, it is justified by pure seeing. Husserl observes: "Wherever we have pure evidence, the pure and direct seeing and grasping of an objectivity itself, we have the same rights, the same certainties. This step provides us with a new objectivity that counts as absolute givenness, the objectivity of essences" (Hua II 8/65).

But if the general is an absolute given, an "immanent" given in the reduced sense of what is seen and grasped in the evidence of pure seeing, even though it does not belong to the real immanence of the *cogitatio* but is situated outside of it, the sense of this "even though" becomes transparent. It is *because* it is not included as one of the real elements of the *cogitatio* and on the condition of not being one of them that the universal essence (and, in particular, the essence of the *cogitatio*) is able to become this absolute given, as the purely seen of a seeing and as an evidence. Through this arrival of the general into pure seeing, a second point can now be proven: the extension of the purely given implies its liberation from the *cogitatio*, its reattachment to evidence, and its *definition as objectivity and no longer as subjectivity*.

This type of given, like that of the universal, is never more pure than when it has become the given of an external reality, a given in and through this exteriority, in and through transcendence. It is no longer necessary to extend absolutely given beyond the *cogitatio*, which would have provided its prototype, but to contrast them radically. Husserl observes: *"It is now no longer obvious and unquestioned that what is absolutely given and what is really immanent are one and the same thing"* (Hua II 9/65). And this remarkable consequence whereby the absolute subjectivity of transcendental life is dispossessed of the original givenness which it carries out in and through itself, in the radical immanence of the *cogitatio*, is its demonstration in the universal where it is seen outside and apart from life as the transcendent given in evidence. Husserl continues: "for the general is absolutely given and yet not really immanent. The knowledge of generalities is itself something singular; it is at any given time a moment in the stream of consciousness. The general itself, which is given in evidence within the stream of consciousness is, on the other hand, not something singular, but rather something general, and thus, in the real [*reellen*] sense, transcendent" (Hua II 9/65–66).

Yet, what does the phenomenological reduction become if its principle is no longer the return to the sphere of the immanence of the *cogitatio* through the putting out of play of everything that, not being included in it and surpassing it in some way, is found to be dubitable in comparison to the certitude residing in the *cogitatio* itself? It must make the reduction, likewise, the object of a radical reworking through which it is no longer an internal element of the *cogitation,* and the *cogitatio* no longer belongs within it as a real element that defines the immanent and is thus undeniable. To the contrary, it becomes the content of a pure seeing placed outside of the *cogitatio* as the intentional correlate of its aim. It constitutes and defines the transcendent as such. After having declared—thereby repeating the essential error—that we have evidence of the *cogitatio* and that this is the reason why the being of the *cogitatio* is an absolute given for us, freed from any problem, the text adds: "Accordingly, the phenomenological reduction does not signify a limitation of the investigation to the real [*reellen*] immanence, to the sphere of what is really [*reell*] contained in the absolute 'this' of the *cogitatio*, but rather the limitation to the sphere of pure self-givenness" (Hua II 60/45). The sphere of absolute givens, now transcendent and no longer immanent, is henceforth totally foreign to the *cogitatio*.

This reversal of the sense of the reduction such that, instead of being a reduction to immanence, it is now a reduction to transcendence and to what is there in front of the conscious regard and consequently outside of consciousness, has been prepared by the distinction between two concepts of immanence that the problem stumbled up against from its initial analyses. This distinction shows Husserl's brilliant instinct for detecting the difficulties of his own thought and solving them in some way before they even appear, which amounts to putting them into complete obscurity. The reduction must choose between these two concepts of immanence. It must clearly say which one of them is the basis for its attempt to produce pure phenomena as well as which one of them is the true nature of pure phenomena, *their phenomenality*. Under the apparent continuity of the investigation, the equivocity of the phenomenological method is to mask the reversal of the sense of the concept of immanence. This reversal points back to the founding structures of being and phenomenology and, as such, should be brought to light. Without having carried out this elucidation, which would have required it to go back to its hither side and to consider its methodological presuppositions, the phenomenological method remains uncertain as to the exact scope of its results, in spite of its rigor and the decisive character of the distinctions it makes use of.

In the passage cited earlier, the equivocity concerns the term *limitation*. It is indeed true, even if we are not yet in a place here to understand why this is the case, that the reduction ought not restrict its theme to the sphere of what, as really included in the *cogitatio*, belongs to its immanent reality and that it ought to take into account the transcendent essences on which the scientific truths it has in sight will be founded. But the "limitation" to one sphere of reality—the immanence of the *cogitatio*—or the extension to another—the transcendence of the universal essence— implies for the investigation an unfounded homogeneity of the means and ends, beyond the distinction between the spheres, in order to be able to know them in spite of their difference. This homogeneity is a presupposition that the phenomenological method harbors and never goes beneath. The homogeneity of the means is pure seeing. The homogeneity of the being to be known is the absolutely given as the seen for this pure seeing. The immanent has become the transcendent. But what does the true immanence, the reality of the *cogitatio* and of life, become? We have already answered this question: it is lost.

The most remarkable feature of the constitution of the general essence that substitutes, in the thematic turn, for the particular *cogitatio* is to confess to this loss and moreover to confront it. The key thesis here is that the pure seeing of the essence of the *cogitatio* is possible in the absence of this *cogitatio*. The existence of the *cogitatio* is therefore unnecessary. The *cogitatio* can be non-given in its reality as a real *cogitatio* and nonetheless its essence can be grasped.

Naturally, if we go back to the hither side of the Husserlian problematic of the reduction and method and ask ourselves about its hidden motives, we can ask: Why will Husserl with extraordinary minutia and an admirable pertinence show that the pure seeing of the essence of the *cogitatio* takes place even when its existence is not given "in person"? The response to this question is given with a striking clarity. It is because the *cogitatio* can be seen as it is only in its immanence that does not break into any separation and in this way does not ever admit any regard to slip into it. It is because absolute subjectivity is the invisible that, if a knowledge of the essence of absolute subjectivity is required, it must occur without the existence of the *cogitatio* and the givenness of its own reality in person. *One must at once have seen the essence of the* cogitatio *and not have seen its reality, its absence.* Because transcendental life refuses to be seen in a gaze and hides its reality from the gaze, the phenomenological method instinctively replaces this reality whose "essence" escapes with a transcendence that is capable of being seen and is being-seen as such. Essence is thus an equivalent, a replacement, a substitute, which is to say that it is the representation of the essential qualities and reality of life in place of their impossible "presentation."

In the absence of the real *cogitatio*, one must construct the theory of the constitution of universal essences and, most importantly, the general essence of the *cogitatio*. This requirement presents us with a difficulty. Is not the general, the genus red for example, constructed on the basis of particular givens for which it appears as the same quality—the red of this ink blotter, of this stuff, and of this sky? Although it is seen in itself and thus as an absolute given in the reduced sense, this does not prevent it from being constituted in an idealizing abstraction which would necessarily have its starting point in these particular givens. In the same way, the pure seeing of the general essence of the *cogitationes* entails the sight of them in their particularity. It involves particular acts of perception, imagination, memory, judgment, and so on. This is why the essences perceived in them are specific essences—of perception, imagination, and the like—before being the essence of the *cogitatio* as such, when what is identical in all these *cogitationes* is recognized and grasped in its reality. But we say that the particular *cogitatio* cannot either be seen or grasped in its reality. If it is the case that the seeing of essences entails the grasping of the particular givens on which it is founded, as it so happens in the grasping of the *cogitationes*, then does not the theory of essences vacillate? This vacillation occurs at the same time as the theory of this constitution of general essences seems to fulfill the possibility of the thematic turn. Instead of being purely and simply able to substitute for the lost reality of the *cogitatio*, the givenness of the essence presupposes it and leads back to it.

The reference back from the essence of the *cogitatio* to the reality of the *cogitatio* can only avoid the pitfall of circularity on the condition that the constitution of the general essence is conceivable on the basis of some givens of the *cogitatio* that would not be givens of its reality, which is to say, would not be the self-givenness of the *cogitatio* in the radical immanence of its immediate and living experience. Suppose that one might have a pure seeing of the essence of the *cogitatio* on the basis of givens playing the role of mere representations of the *cogitatio*, for example, images. By forming the image of a perception, an act of remembering, imagining, and so forth and by using these images as basic particular givens for the idealizing act of abstraction, one would be able to carry out this abstraction and to perceive, in a *clara et distincta perceptio*, the essence of perception, the essence of memory, or the essence of the imagination. As the identical element shared by a plurality of perceptions, memories, and images, the general essence of these intentions presupposes the giving of this plurality. The pure seeing of their specific essences will be constructed on the basis of the plurality of *cogitationes*. But is it not the nature of the imagination to be free and to be able to provide as many particular givens as one would like of these particular *cogitationes* whose essence one seeks to determine? Moreover, by freely forming these givens and by endowing them with every conceivable or *imaginable* quality, fiction marks the dividing line between those that are necessary to the internal constitution of the "thing" and those without which it is still possible, that is, between the essential characteristics and the accidental or contingent ones. The eidetic in phenomenology—notably the theory of eidetic analysis as resting on free fantasy—is the palliative conceived by Husserl to confront a difficulty that determines his thought from the outset. By founding itself solely on evidence and pure seeing, it makes a rigorous science and an eidetics of absolute subjectivity possible, even though in principle absolute subjectivity slips away from every grasp of this kind.

But the theory of essences is developed within the framework of the reduction with whose presuppositions it conforms in every respect. It does not suffice that essences are seen in a pure seeing and thus are seen as pure phenomena or absolute givens. It is also necessary that the particular givens, on the basis of which the general will be perceived as their shared identity, are themselves seen and perceived as they really are. They must be given in person; they must be absolute givens in the reduced sense, which is to say in pure seeing. When the *cogitationes* have been replaced by their images, are the particular givens that must serve as the basis for the constitution of general essences still absolute givens? Do images, which are only explicitly representations and present the *cogitationes* in their absence and no longer in their presence, still give the *cogitationes* in their reality?

This can be the case on only one condition, namely, that the image is still seen and that, as the given for a pure seeing, it offers itself likewise as an absolute given. In order to maintain the validity of self-givenness, the givenness of reality in itself, in person, when the reality is not there, Husserl will confer a meaning to the extension of pure seeing which is so radical that it will shake crucial distinctions on which phenomenology explicitly rests. If, in abandoning the *cogitatio*, one is confined to seeing and what is seen in it, is not everything seen in the same way, insofar as it is seen? In the still undetermined given, the reduction makes an attempt to draw a boundary line that separates what is really seen—the immanent—and distinguishes it from everything that is only presumed, simply intended, emptily intended without really being given. But is not the simply intended, if one considers it solely as intended, also given and also seen in some way, without which it would be nothing at all in this phenomenology of seeing? The separation between the given of pure seeing and the simply intended becomes difficult when the intended is seen in its own way. The strict boundary, which the reduction gives apodictically in order to be able to begin its theoretical work of elucidation, appears to be permeable. The radical distinctions become fluid.

First of all, there is a blurring of the distinction between the seen and the simply intended. The reduction sought to arrive at "the immanent ... characterized by the phenomenological reduction" and in this way: "I mean precisely what is immanent, not what it refers to beyond itself," and thus one is able "to see what is to be seen here, namely, the distinction between the quasi-givenness of transcendent objects and the absolute givenness of the phenomenon itself" (Hua II 45/34–35). But when the "absolute givenness of the phenomenon itself" is a first transcendence, the seen of a seeing, and the quasi-givenness of the transcendent object is in the end nothing different, then the difference between the given and the quasi-given becomes blurred. That is because they are both something "seen" and because they both belong to a same dimension of presence, namely, exteriority and the finitude that is tied to it. And while the analysis of the absolute given has had no other effect than to give evidence of its precariousness as the immanent given of the consciousness of internal time, inversely, the analysis of the quasi-given, constrained to show how this quasi-given is all the while a given, has recognized it likewise as the seen of seeing. As a result, every difference between the seen and the intended is absolutely abolished.

In total defeat, the fifth lecture concedes gradually but unavoidably that everything seen has the same right, whether it is an immanent given of the reduction or the transcendent object and any one of its aspects—imaginary, emptily intended, and so on—provided that it has one. Then it is stopped short of breath before a piece of evidence: the homogeneity of the field of being as determined completely by transcendence and defined by it. Here are the crucial moments of this confession. In the perception of a mundane object—for example, a house—the reduction has privileged the immanent phenomenon of the house, the sense data in which it appears and that are themselves constituted in phenomenological time. Husserl asks, "But is it not also evident that a house appears in the house-phenomenon, thus giving us a reason to call it a house-perception? Furthermore, is it not just a house in general, but this house, determined in such and such a way and appearing with just these determinations?" (Hua II 72/53). The transcendent object, as a *cogitatum*, and not only the immanent given is an evident given. This is true not only for the object of perception but also for every possible object that is seen, for example, an imaginary object. Husserl observes: "And when I call forth a fiction in my imagination, so that, say, before me St. George the knight is killing a dragon, is it not evident that I the imagined phenomenon represents precisely St. George . . . as something transcendent?" (ibid.).

It is not just intuitive thought in all its forms, for example, the imaginary, which gives itself to be seen and is thus something seen and which, insofar as it is limited to the seen, escapes from being challenged. Nonintuitive or symbolic thought, the thought that emptily intends, also proposes what it intends as a phenomenon and thus escapes from doubt. Husserl notes: "Without any intuition, I think '2 times 2 is 4.' Can I doubt that I am thinking about this numerical proposition?" (Hua II 73/53). And this holds as well for the completely absurd, which, as a transcendent object and a *cogitatum*, "can also be given." In all of these cases, "an intentional object is obviously there" (ibid.).

This sudden validation of every form of transcendent presence, the presence of an absurd being just as much as an imaginary object or a perceived one, but always the presence of some object, leads us far away from the reduction that wanted to remain strictly within the sphere of immanence. Husserl becomes aware right away of this deviation from the fundamental criteria of phenomenology:

> Now we should not maintain that what we have cited in this last series of considerations is given in the genuine sense of actual givenness. Otherwise it would turn out that anything perceived, imagined, pretended, or symbolically represented, every fiction and absurdity would be "given with evidence." We only want to point out *the great difficulties that lie here.*" (Hua II 73/53–54)

Whatever the difficulties may be and however Husserl aims to resolve them (by holding firmly to evidence and by constructing a systematic theory of the various types of intentionality and thus a phenomenology devoted exclusively to problems of constitution), the validation of the imaginary given as something seen makes the constitution of the general essence possible and, in particular, the essence that is of interest to us—

the essence of thought. It suffices that the *cogitationes* serving as the basis for the process of ideation be given, or *be given in their absence*, even when their reality slips away. This is precisely what they are as imaginary. Husserl works to establish, in such minute detail, the phenomenological validity of the image so that it too is an absolute given and so that the constitution of the *cogitatio*'s essence on the basis of imagined *cogitationes* has a validity satisfying the reduction.

The demonstration is made with the example of color. If I consider an imagined but not sensed color, it is nonetheless something before the conscious regard. "It is in a certain way given: it stands before my gaze" (Hua II 69/51). It thus suffices to reduce it as one reduces a sensed color, to no longer consider it as the imagined color of an ink blotter or a house but as itself, in order to be in the presence of the "phenomenon" of an imagined color and to take it "just as I 'see' it, as I 'experience' it" (ibid.). Put another way, Husserl observes, "It appears and appears itself; it presents itself [*sie erscheint und erscheint selbst, sie stellt sich selbst dar*]; in an act of seeing it in its representation I can make judgments about it and about the moments that constitute it and their interconnections" (ibid.)

But, to make judgments about perceived moments, for example, in the imagined color, about the relations between these moments, about the ones that are necessary for something to be a color and about those that are not, and finally about the basis of the givenness of these imagined moments and their necessary interconnections, to perceive the essence of the color, which is nothing but the necessary interconnections between these moments, it is precisely to have pure seeing of the individual essence of the color in the absence of every consideration having to do with a real color and its existence. For what holds for the essence of color also holds for all essences in general and specifically for the essences of the *cogitationes* whose reality was lost by phenomenology but that, however, continue to be given in person as imaginary givens. On the basis of these imaginary but absolute givens, the constitution of their essences can be brought about.

Indifference toward existence—the existence of particular givens on the basis of which the pure seeing of their essences, through ideational abstraction, functions—is the leitmotif of the Husserlian theory of the constitution of general essences and the key presupposition of the phenomenological method as an eidetic method. In the fifth lecture, it is categorically affirmed several times: "The essence of the phenomenological tone quality, tone intensity, the tone of colors, brightness, and the like, is itself given even if the ideating abstraction occurs on the basis of a perception or on the basis of a representation in imagination. The actual positing of existence, or the modification of that positing, is in both cases irrelevant" (Hua II 68/50). Husserl continues: "The instances must stand before our eyes, but not in the same way that states of affairs do in perception. In a consideration of essence, perception and imaginative representation are entirely equivalent—the same essence can be seen in both, can be abstracted in both, the positing of existence in each case being irrelevant" (ibid.). And again: "It is, moreover, clear that even if the underlying instances are given in perceptions, *it is precisely that which lends distinction to the givenness of perception—namely, existence—that has no bearing on the matter*" (Hua II 69/50). It no longer matters that in the case of the aforementioned perception of a particular *cogitatio*, the existence of the *cogitatio* slips away in reality from the pure seeing of this perception. This is no longer an obstacle to the constitution of the essence of the *cogitatio*, since this constitution functions equally on the basis of either an imaginary given or a real given, the latter of which is indeed lacking in the case of the *cogitatio*.

In this way, the phenomenological method and phenomenology in general are once again possible, even though their founding principle, the givenness in person of the *cogitatio*, has drifted away. Two conditions were required to save them from shipwreck. The first was the thematic turn in which the invisible reality of the *cogitatio* is replaced with its transcendent essence which is offered to a seeing. The second was that the particular *cogitationes* that must serve as givens for the constitution of their transcendent essence remain absolute givens even when they escape from the sight of the reduction. Behind the illusory reach of the concept of self-givenness, it was thus necessary for their givenness in images to be posited as equivalent to the givenness of their reality and, avowedly or not, for the sacrifice of reality to be carried out.

Husserl did not misunderstand the radical opposition between the reality of the *cogitatio* and its irreal noematic correlate, specifically, the ideality of essence. By retrieving this central insight from the Cartesian *cogito*, he in fact gave it its full meaning. From this, there results an undeniable disqualification of the transcendent being to the degree that it is situated outside of transcendental life and is deprived of the true reality defined by and coinciding with transcendental life. In this respect, one can say that every philosophy of transcendence, which limits itself to the knowledge and the understanding of transcendent being alone, is a philosophy of death. In contrast with his successors, this is not the case for Husserl. Even when he explicitly takes the intentional object as his guiding thread, the constitution of the intentional object is the true theme of the investigation. Transcendent being thus only exists through reference to this transcendental life from which it draws its possibility and on the condition that it is each time the noema of a noesis. And yet, despite the continual reference to the most profound reality of the *cogitatio* understood as the source of every conceivable being, as the proto-givenness, and as the original phenomenalizing of phenomenality, Husserlian phenomenology will undo what should have constituted its basic theme. This is already evidenced in the 1907 lectures' analysis of the reality of the *cogitatio*.

In keeping with the thematic displacement analyzed in detail before, it is always directed toward the essence instead of the reality of the *cogitatio*. Through a pure seeing, it seeks to grasp the general features that make the *cogitatio* be what it is. Ultimately, it is not this displacement as such that calls for critique. Phenomenology is a mode of thought in the sense of an activity of knowledge. It functions as a seeing, necessarily obeying an immanent teleology of seeing as well as the *a priori* laws and limitations that define its sphere of activity. What matters is the way in which, in favor of this displacement that thematizes the essence of the *cogitatio*, the most essential feature of this essence comprising the reality of the *cogitatio*—its existence—is completely overshadowed.

What does Husserl actually see when, in the pure seeing of the reduction, he considers, either on the basis of presentational or representational givens, what particular *cogitationes* have in common? And in their shared identity, what element does he retain as the most important? In the reality of the *cogitatio* thus represented to the phenomenologist in its ideal essence, this feature is the *cogitatio*'s relation to an object. The object was put out of play by the reduction as something surpassing what is really seen in the seeing that thematizes the reality of the *cogitatio*. The "relating-to" underlies every *cogitatio* as that which gives it a power of manifestation. In this way, the famous definition of consciousness as "consciousness of something," intentionality, and transcendence is established. This "relating-to" is indeed a real element of the *cogitatio*, which, like the *hyle*, is one of its internal and immanent components, in contrast with everything that is situated outside itself, every transcendent element. By taking into view the immanent layer of the elements really inherent to the *cogitatio* and comprising its reality, Husserl finds nothing but transcendence, that is to say "relating-to" as the capacity to relate to every possible object and to everything that can be a phenomenon for us.

Following Husserl on this point, we said that the second sense of the concept of immanence, which refers to the givens in the consciousness of internal time and so to a first objectification of transcendental life, corresponds to the concept of transcendence understood in its first sense. We now see that the original sense, the first sense, of this concept of immanence would indeed be equivalent to the first sense of the concept of transcendence, if it were true that the immanent reality of the *cogitatio* were its "relating-to," and so if it were intentionality and transcendence as such.

The analysis of the essence of the *cogitatio*'s "essential" contribution to reality is the interpretation of the *cogitatio* as transcendence. Speaking about mental processes reduced to absolute givens which "are intentionally related to objective reality," the third lecture states, "this *relatedness* is a characteristic that resides *in* them" (Hua II 45/34; trans. modified). With respect to the essence of knowledge, which consists of the ability to enter into relation with an object, it is affirmed in the same way: "The relation to something transcendent, whether I question the existence of the transcendent object or the ability of the relation to make contact with it, still contains something that can be apprehended within the pure phenomenon. The relating-itself-to-something-transcendent . . . is an inner characteristic of the phenomenon" (Hua II 46/35). Likewise, the fourth lecture states, "It belongs to the essence of cognitive experiences to have an *intention*; they refer to something; they relate themselves in one way or another to an objectivity. *This 'relating itself to an objectivity' belongs to them* even if objectivity does not" (Hua II 55/41). How, then, can one say that with the thematic displacement and the taking into consideration of the essence of the *cogitatio*, the reality of the *cogitatio*, its immanent reality with its real components, is lost?

Husserl thinks of the reality of the *cogitatio* as transcendence. In and through the "relating-to" that is constitutive of its reality, the *cogitatio* is intentionally directed toward the object and, in the transcendence of this intentionality, gives it to be seen, makes it manifest, and reveals it. Here revelation is the revelation of the object. Appearing is the appearing of the object in the sense that what appears is the object and also in the sense that since appearing is the object, the mode of appearing implied in this appearing is the mode of appearing belonging to the object, its way of being shown by becoming an object, that is, objectivity as such. But what is the mode of appearing of this "relating-to"?

There is no response to this question either in Husserlian phenomenology or in the philosophical development that follows it. In place of this response, which could only amount to a redefinition of the concept of the phenomenon and so of phenomenology itself, one finds a type of evasion and, more profoundly, an illusion. The situation is actually as follows: there is no mode of revelation of "relating-to" in itself and as such. But, in the phenomenological reduction and the ideation that extends it, the phenomenologist sees in a pure seeing that "relating-to" belongs to the essence of the *cogitatio* and that it is a real element of the *cogitatio*. So the pure seeing in the reduction sees the "relating-to" and offers itself as the illusory response to the unanswered question: how is "relating-to" revealed in itself? The gaze that sees "relating-to" takes the place of the revelation of this "relating-to" and passes itself off for it. "Relating-to" is a real element of the *cogitatio*. And if one were to retain only that, then one would say that it is the real element of the *cogitatio*. One would say that the *cogitatio* or consciousness is this "relating-to;" it is pure transcendence and nothing else.

Like Heidegger in the *Zähringen* seminar, one would renounce the very word "consciousness" insofar as it seems to retain the idea of immanence, a "being-inside" consciousness, which would thus be something other than the pure ek-static bursting forth and the "there" of an "outside" which is defined by this outside. Husserl will be praised for having "saved the object" but will be deplored for the fact that this would be accomplished by "putting it in the immanence of consciousness."[7] How can one fail to see that, from the first explicit definition of the reduction in the 1907 lectures, with the sliding of the sense of the concept of immanence, the "being-inside" consciousness as an intentional inherence refers to nothing but the "there" of the "outside" that *Dasein* seeks to think? How can one fail to see that, instead of being different in the two cases, the sense of the word "being," the *sein* in *Bewusst-sein* and in *Da-sein*, is in fact the same, if this is a matter of referring to phenomenality as such.

By substituting the pure gaze in which the phenomenologist sees the "relating-to" for its self-givenness in the original *cogitatio*, phenomenology does not only trace the limits of its future possibilities but also goes to the end of its illusion. What exactly is pure seeing? To see something is to be intentionally related to it. So "relating-to" is given as the absolute, as the alpha and the omega of phenomenality. In the phenomenological reduction and the grasp of the *cogitatio*'s essence it provides, "relating-to" is two-sided. The reduction is the pure seeing of the *cogitatio*'s essence, "relating-to" this essence. And what does one see in this pure gaze as the essence and reality of the *cogitatio*? One sees this "relating-to." Thus, the circle is perfect. In the reduction, thought is related to itself on the basis of what it is: a "relating-to." This circle is the illusion that, closing onto itself, casts a shadow over what it lacks and constantly presupposes. What is lacking in this reflexive circle when "relating-to" is related to itself? Nothing less than the possibility of this "relating-to" as such.

This possibility is phenomenological. The "relating-to" is phenomenological. Phenomenologically, to be "relating-to" is to see. To say that the "relating-to" is not its own phenomenological possibility means, in a rigorous way, that *seeing does not see itself.* This means that seeing is not a phenomenon in and of itself. A seeing that would only see would be a phenomenological nothing; it would see nothing. There is only seeing if, in an unperceived way, seeing is more than itself. There always acts within it a power other than its own, a power in which it is auto-affected so that it feels its seeing and feels itself seeing. In this way, we should not say that "we see" (*videmus*) but, like Descartes, "we feel our seeing" (*sentimus nos videre*). This auto-affection is the original phenomenality, the original givenness as a self-givenness, for example, the self-givenness of seeing to itself.

This self-givenness, however, is structurally different from "relating-to." It is not in itself a "relating-to" but insurmountably excludes it from itself. It is not outside of itself but in itself, not transcendence but radical immanence. And it is only on the basis of this radical immanence that something like transcendence is possible. Seeing is actualized only as a nonseeing, by not being related to itself in an act of seeing and by not revealing itself through this and thus as something unseen and invisible. This nonseeing, this unseen, this invisible, is not the unconscious. It is not the negation of phenomenality but its first phenomenalization. It is not a presupposition but rather our life in its non-ek-static but yet undeniable pathos. Only the affect in its passion is undeniable. If the question of phenomenology, which alone can define itself, is the question of the givenness not of objects but of their how, then only the theme of radical immanence as transcendental affectivity will allow it to complete its agenda. For this radical how is what phenomenology misses at the very moment when it explicitly defines itself for the first time.

Why does phenomenology miss this? Because it is conceived as a method. It is clear that method derives from thought, being only a mere exercise of thought in accordance with procedures which have been carefully elaborated and whose results are assured. Having become a method, however, phenomenology no longer knows the phenomenality in which thought moves, that it presupposes, and to which it is confided. Philosophy, since its Greek origin at any rate, is confined to this phenomenality of thought. Its use in systematic processes of elaboration and elucidation does not allow reflection to escape from the constraining power of its finite horizon: "the horizon of being." Instead, thought is irremediably enclosed in this horizon, insofar as in reflection it is only the duplication of this space of light and its finitude: the seeing of the act of seeing. One can indeed challenge this reflection and thus the reduction itself, but one is only confined more strictly to the field in which they operate and to the transcendence that, since its first formulation, the reduction had substituted for life. The overwhelming truth of this central connection between the phenomenological method and Greek phenomenality as well as the essential limitation of the investigation that results from it is illustrated nowhere better than in the famous §7 of *Being and Time*.

The issue there is to elucidate the method of the investigation that inquires into the being of beings. The meaning of being in general is the theme of this work, understanding that it is "things" which are in question and that the "things themselves" must determine their manner of treatment. This manner of treatment is phenomenological. The concept of phenomenology must be understood through the elements that make it up. Hence, the paragraph is divided in three parts (A, B, C), which treat the "phenomenon," the "*logos*," and the "phenomenology," respectively.

The first two parts are constructed in similar ways. A fundamental sense, for the "phenomenon" as well as the "*logos*," is defined in respect to which all the other uses of these basic concepts are shown to be mere derivatives, so that the fundamental sense alone matters. And this occurs even though the analysis of the derivative senses prevails a great deal over the fundamental sense, so that the analysis of the fundamental sense seems succinct, poor, and too quick with respect to the decisive nature of its implications. More seriously, it seems that if we look more closely there is neither explicitly a conceptual nor a phenomenological analysis but rather a philological examination. The problem is one of knowing what the words *phenomenon* and *logos* mean in Greek. A mere factual and historical consideration is what serves as the basis for the definition of phenomenology and ontology, insofar as ontology refers to phenomenology. The introduction to §7 concludes by saying that "the history of the word [phenomenology] itself, which originated presumably from the Wolffian school, is not important here" (SZ 28/25). Yet, it is through history, and moreover, through a limited period of history, that this thought, which claims to be a phenomenological thinking of being, will be completely determined.

The philological analysis of the Greek word *phenomenon* can be broken down into two parts. The first is limited to indicating that the term derives from the Greek verb *phainesthai*, meaning "to show itself." So, the phenomenon is what shows itself, the showing of itself, the manifest (*das was sich zeigt, das Sichzeigende, das Offenbare*). At this stage, the concept of the phenomenon adopts a purely formal meaning, the phenomenality to which it refers remains wholly undetermined. It is what allows everything that is shown to be shown, to appear, and to phenomenalize by becoming a phenomenon, without anything being said about the phenomenological nature of this pure phenomenality as such.

This formal phase of the analysis of the word *phenomenon* only lasts an instant. It is quickly covered over or, better, submerged under a material interpretation that will provide pure phenomenality with a specific content, a particular nature, a phenomenological materiality by which phenomenality no longer refers to the mere fact of appearing in an undetermined way. This passage from the formal to the material meaning of the word *phenomenon* is a passage by which this word becomes a concept and indeed a fundamental phenomenological concept. This passage happens so quickly that it is important to pause there and to examine it with care. One can then see that it is made up of two movements. The first is the movement by which one slips from the consideration of the phenomenon, of what appears (*was sich zeigt*) to the act of appearing perceived in itself (*phainesthai*). This slippage is central, because it is constitutive of phenomenology. Phenomenology takes as its theme not what appears but the manner in which it appears, that is, appearing as such. It is precisely due to this thematic displacement that the second movement is surreptitiously accomplished in Heidegger's text. The second movement is the one in which pure appearing, considered in its purity, receives a radical material determination. It no longer refers to the fact of appearing in general but to a particular mode of the fulfillment of appearing in and through which appearing gets an important restriction. This restriction to a specific mode of appearing is also a restriction of phenomenology and ontology themselves. It is remarkable that precisely when it defines itself in the thematic sliding from what appears to appearing, phenomenology is submitted unconsciously to this same restriction. This occurs even though its introductory analyses are not purely or strictly phenomenological but philological.

The Greek word *phainesthai* does not signify a pure appearing, freed from every presupposition and independent from the way it is said in a place or a language. If this were so, it would be this pure appearing and it alone which would dictate to us—*in its actual and original mode of fulfillment and according to a saying that would be nothing but this mode of fulfillment and this how of appearing*—what appearing is in its concrete appearing, in the phenomenological materiality of its pure phenomenality, when nothing but this appears. *Phainesthai* means precisely the type of appearing expressed in *phainesthai*. It is the middle-voice construction of *phaino*, which means to bring into daylight, to put in the light (*an den Tag bringen, in die Helle stellen*). Its Greek root is *pha* or *phos*, which signifies light or brightness, "that is, that within which something can become manifest, visible in itself" (*d.h. das, worin etwas offenbar, an ihm selbst sichtbar warden kann*) (SZ 28/25). Understood now in this restricted way—in this Greek way—appearing thus refers to the light and the brightness illuminating every thing. Under this illumination and in this light, every thing becomes visible and in this sense a phenomenon. To put it another way, appearing proposes itself henceforth as a horizon of visibility within which everything that is capable of becoming visible and becoming a phenomenon does so.

From this very unique interpretation of the concept of appearing borrowed from both common sense and Greek, there follows the distinction between appearing and what appears, or to express it in the Husserlian terminology of the 1907 lectures, between givenness and the given. What appears only appears in and through the work of appearing. In this sense, what appears differs from appearing *in the same way that what is illuminated differs from the light which illuminates it*. Light, for example, is always the same, while what it illuminates can vary indefinitely. But what appears only differs from appearing because appearing is difference as such, because the light only illuminates what is different from it, what is put before it at a distance and outside of it. This happens even though light only gives its brightness in the illumination constituted by this Outside, in such a way that what is illuminated, what appears, always stands outside and at a distance. The phenomenon, understood as what is held at a distance and "shines in the light," is for Heidegger what the Greeks called a being. Appearing, which allows a being to be shown and to be manifest by showing itself, is being in contrast with beings.

After having shown that all of the other uses of the concept of the phenomenon point back to the fundamental meaning in which the phenomenon is what can become visible in the light, part A of §7 concludes: "But if in the way we grasp the concept of the phenomenon we leave undetermined which beings are to be addressed as phenomena, and if we leave altogether open whether the self-showing is actually a particular being or a characteristic of the being of beings, then we are dealing solely with the formal concept of the phenomenon" (SZ 31/27). Though brief, it is clear that the determination of the phenomenon as what shows itself in the light is anything but formal. Whatever may be the complexity of the explanations and the many forms of elucidation that it calls for, these will only serve to explain what is implied in the initial and huge presupposition according to which showing itself means becoming visible in the light and thus in the "there" of an outside and thus in the world.

If the crucial question of phenomenology and consequently of ontology were the question of life, and if the mode by which it became a phenomenological essence as living were such as to exclude in principle every presentation in the light of a world, then this so-called formal characterization of the concept of the phenomenon would have already have situated us beyond the essential and the mere possibility of ever reaching it. The situation encountered by Husserl in the 1907 lectures would become markedly aggravated here, because the mere project of grasping life, once perceived as the Cartesian *cogitatio*, would no longer surface for thought. The investigation was blocked by a chance encounter with beings and their conditions, conditions from which our ownmost being has already been removed.

The banality of the mundane presupposition of the concept of the phenomenon—"phenomenon" as something showing itself in a world—leads to the question posed for the first time in the 1907 lectures and taken up again in the introduction of §7 of *Being and Time*, namely, the question of the specificity of its phenomenological usage, "phenomena in the phenomenological sense." In the 1907 lectures, the reduction accounts for this specificity; it is the radicalization of seeing; the decision to be confined to "immanent" seeing frees it from triviality. §7, which goes without the reduction and rejects the "immanence" of consciousness, borrows its response to this question from the thematics suggested by Kant. In what appears, in the phenomenon in the ordinary sense, phenomenology thematizes appearing, its pure modalities, such as the forms of Kantian intuition, for example. These pure modalities of appearing are "the phenomena of phenomenology." But this grandiose and important project due to which phenomenology would have to open an entirely new field of investigation loses its revolutionary power once the appearing thematically intended and recognized by it is only that of the ordinary, mundane phenomenon. While this cannot be taken in the naïve way as what appears without its appearing ever being a problem, it nonetheless sets out the essential limitation to the investigation. This is made even more evident in Part B, which is dedicated to the concept of the *logos*.

Here once again, the derivative uses of the concept—reason (in the dual sense of *Vernunft* and *Grund*), judgment, definition, relation, and so on—must be set aside in order to take hold of its fundamental meaning as speech. Understood in its first content as the Greek *deloun*, the role of speech is "to make manifest what one is being talked about in speech" (*offenbar machen das, wovon in der Rede die Rede ist*) (SZ 32/28). *Logos* thus "lets something be seen [*phainesthai*], namely what is being talked about," and it makes it seen to the one who speaks as well as those to whom one speaks (ibid.). It is speech thus understood in the Aristotelian way as *apophansis*. What is said is drawn from what is being talked about, and in this way spoken communication makes manifest what it is talking about and thereby makes it accessible to others. That is why the fact "of making manifest, in the sense of letting something be seen by indicating it" is placed at its center and constitutes its essence (ibid.). It is precisely because *logos* is letting something be seen that, for Heidegger, it can be true with a truth that points back to the original truth and presupposes it. For, the being-true of the *logos* consists of its ability to take the beings that are talked about out of their concealment and to let them be seen outside of their concealment [*alethes*] and to disclose them. To the extent that it discloses beings by speaking about them, it is true that the *logos* is only a specific mode of letting something be seen and thus only a specific mode of the truth. Truth in the original sense is *aisthesis*, "the simple sense perception of something" (SZ 33/29). With its role being to make the beings that are talked about seen, the fact remains that the *logos* involves this collection of beings in perception and thus in truth in the original sense.

As Part C of §7 will do, it now suffices to collect and compare the fundamental meanings of the concepts *phenomenon* and *logos* in order to establish in a rigorous way what phenomenology is and should be. This comparison will put before our eyes a crucial piece of evidence that Part C indicates from the outset. It will determine, sometimes consciously and sometimes unconsciously, not just the entire paragraph but also the entire work. Heidegger states: "When we bring to mind concretely what has been exhibited in the interpretation of 'phenomenon' and 'logos,' we are struck by an inner relation between what is meant by these terms" (SZ 34/30). This relation is so intimate that it is much more than a mere relation. It is an essential identity, which is to say the essence of phenomenality reduced to the phenomenality of the world. There is indeed a dissymmetry between the two terms: the phenomenon or rather phenomenality refers to the object of phenomenology; the *logos*, which is the way of treating the phenomenon, the mode of knowing which should be applied to such an object, is the type of science or method which is adequate to its grasp. But it has been shown that the *logos*—whether it is understood in a restrictive modern way, as knowledge, science, and method or in its original content as speech and thus as letting what speech talks about be seen in speech—can only be carried out, at any rate, on the basis of this letting-be-seen, which is to say ultimately on the basis of pure phenomenality as such. For what Parts A and B have shown and Part C gathers together is that the phenomenality implied in every speech and *a fortiori* in every knowledge, science, and method is precisely the same as the phenomenality of the phenomenon in general, a phenomenality interpreted in the Greek way. Conversely, this means that *the essence of phenomenality in general is the essence of speech and thought*. Idealism, this traditional philosophical view in which reality is reduced to the knowledge that we can have of it in language and thought, is the hidden presupposition of this supposedly new beginning.

The second paragraph of Part C takes up in a negative way the question of the definition of phenomenology by considering it as a *logos* and a method but not in terms of its object. Heidegger writes: "'Phenomenology' neither designates the object of its researches nor is it a title that describes their content. The word only tells us something about the how of the demonstration and treatment of what this discipline considers" (SZ 35/30). What does the phenomenology of this how affirm about this way of treating what it treats? It affirms precisely what the 1907 lectures said, which is to say that one must methodically restrict oneself to what is really seen, really given, by setting aside everything which goes beyond this immediate given. This is what Part C explains in the following way: "Science 'of' the phenomena means that it grasps its objects in such a way that everything about them to be discussed must be directly indicated and directly elucidated" (ibid.). This repetition of the Husserlian methodological presupposition which prohibits every transcendent construction—"insisting that we avoid all non-demonstrative determinations"—is accompanied with a remark presented as a simple restatement and thus as something self-evident: "The basically tautological expression 'descriptive phenomenology' has the same sense" (ibid.).

But on what conditions is the expression "descriptive phenomenology" tautological? First, it is tautological on the condition that the concept of phenomenology is taken in a purely methodological sense. Description refers to making something come into evidence and to the "direct indication" in a process of thought that belongs not only to phenomenology but also ultimately to every scientific investigation whatever. But, the concept of phenomenology cannot be taken in a purely methodological sense, if it is true that it does not only refer to the *logos* but also to the phenomenon and if the *logos* is possible only on the basis of phenomenality. If phenomenology also implies the phenomenon on which the *logos* depends and that determines it throughout, then the expression "phenomenological description" can only be tautological under a second condition. This condition would hold that the essence of the phenomenality implied in the *logos* and the *phenomenon* is in fact the same—that is to say, on the condition that the appearing in which thought moves also refers to every conceivable appearing and to the how of every phenomenon whatsoever. What determines every possible experience for us is what we experience in and through thought, according to its way of operating, more broadly than in speech, in making manifest what belongs to the saying of this speech. This analysis aims to be very simple and presuppositionless; it proceeds by direct indication on the basis of the two basic parts of the word *phenomenology*. Yet, once again, it puts before our eyes a presupposition that is all the more constrictive because it remains unthought. This presupposition is that there is only type of appearing, the very same one that reigns and spreads through the *logos* of speech and thought.

Restricting itself to this sole presupposition, Part C does not avoid contradiction, however. After having claimed that phenomenology "does not designate the object of its researches" but a certain way of treating the object, a description, the second paragraph adds: "The character of description itself, the specific sense of the *logos*, can be established only from the 'material content' [*Sachheit*] of what is 'described,' that is, of what is to be brought to scientific determinateness in the way phenomena are encountered" (SZ 35/31). It is now the object or the phenomenon that is important. In and through its own phenomenality and showing itself directly there, the phenomenon is also what enables the method to restrict itself to direct indication. Is that to say that, due to this restriction, appearing regains its rights and will dictate to phenomenology, understood as a method, the mode of treatment that should be applied to it?

But what appearing would dictate a method to phenomenology and determine its *logos*? The very same one that dwells in the *logos* and that allows it to make manifest what it speaks about: the appearing of the perceived thing, of the worldly being. The most trivial and superficial concept of the phenomenon, purely and simply borrowed from ordinary perception, serves as the basis for the *logos* and the phenomenality that defines all of phenomenology. Heidegger adds: "The meaning of the formal and common concepts of the phenomenon formally justifies our calling every way of indicating beings as they show themselves in themselves 'phenomenology'" (ibid.).

Here the essential identity between the phenomenon's essence and the description that is proposed to discover it in its truth becomes clear, to such a degree that there is no longer any way to distinguish them from one another. The indication of the being as it shows itself defines and constitutes the method, thus stripping it of every possibly utility. "Phenomenology" does not refer to anything more than the most ordinary experience. There is a phenomenology of everything and anything, if it is permissible to call "every way of indicating beings . . . phenomenology" (ibid.). Coming up against the triviality of this mundane definition of phenomenology for the third time, §7 must for the third time ask the question of the specificity of the phenomenon of phenomenology and at the same time the question of the origin or simply the reason for phenomenology. Heidegger asks: "Now what must be taken into account if the formal concept of phenomenon is to be deformalized to the phenomenological one, and how does this differ from the common concept? What is it that phenomenology is to 'let be seen'?" (ibid.).

The answer, in the end, is letting-be-seen. The thematization of appearing here receives a more systematic and deliberate form than in Husserl. Moreover, by placing concealment at the heart of truth, Heidegger believes himself to give phenomenology a motivation, for if something "does not show itself initially and for the most part," then elucidation is necessary (ibid.). This does not alter in any way their shared presupposition, which is the essential identity of the phenomenon and the *logos* based on the prior Greek understanding of them. That is to say on the basis of this interpretation, *the object and the method of phenomenology are identical*. Thus we are brought back to the central question that guides our present inquiry.

The identity of the object and the method of phenomenology seem self-evident for a number of reasons that surface in §7. If the object of phenomenology is indeed appearing and if appearing "belongs to what initially and for the most part shows itself," what method is appropriate here if not one which is founded on appearing and devoted entirely to it? (ibid.). Method always designates the means of access to the object insofar as this means is the best one or, more radically, the only one possible. What can found any access to the object whatsoever if not the appearing in and through which this object is shown to us? The means of access is the method itself; it is thus the phenomenality of the phenomenon to which it has access. But if the object of phenomenology is not a determinate phenomenon, a this or a that, but rather this phenomenality as such which allows particular phenomena to be, then the path of access to it is in no way different from itself. Pure phenomenality in its actual phenomenalization is given to us, thus clearing the path that leads to it. Phenomenality is the path and the access of the method. The path of access to the phenomenon is the phenomenon itself, its phenomenality. Thus the object of phenomenology and its method are the same, because the former (appearing) constitutes the path that the latter (the method) need only follow. It is this "path."

This identity between the object and the method of phenomenology loses its evidence once phenomenology abandons formalism—in which the seemingly most important intuitions remain marked with a deep-seated uncertainty—and becomes material. With rigor, it then attempts to say phenomenologically what makes up the phenomenality of this pure phenomenality. As our critique of §7 has shown, one must recognize that, instead of being formal, the Heideggerian concept of the phenomenon is constructed on a presupposition that gives it a specific sense. According to this material presupposition, the "phenomenon" is what shows itself in the light, and likewise, this presupposition determines the *logos* inasmuch as the manifestation that it brings about is "letting something be seen by showing it" and so implies the phenomenon in the Greek sense of the *phainomenon*. What accounts for the identity between the phenomenon and the *logos* is no longer an indeterminate concept of appearing; it is the visibility cited twice above—both in the phenomenon and in the *logos*.

If, to the contrary, life is the original appearing in the pathetic immediacy of its self-appearing, which thus founds every possible appearing and thus every phenomenon, and if it escapes from the domain of the visible, and if, as this original appearing, this transcendental life actually is the object of phenomenology, then the identity between the object and method of phenomenology is broken abruptly. It would give way to a heterogeneity so radical that it is first presented to thought as an abyss. The *logos* must speak by letting the essence of phenomenality be seen in what it says. Instead of being able to rely on this and to bear it as its own way of being seen, life would differ completely from the *logos*, since life, as the original essence of phenomenality, necessarily excludes from itself every possible instance of letting something be seen.

At the same time, the method regains a sense and phenomenology as a method regains its own rights. It is no longer the sorry tautology that is limited to repeating, in a useless duplication, the immediate phenomenon, the indication of beings, and that is identified with this indication that gives us access to the phenomenon by tracing the path and the method to follow in order to attain it. Quite the contrary, the object and method of phenomenology are opposed to one another phenomenologically as two irreconcilable essences: as the non-ek-static and pathetic revelation of life, on one hand, and as the letting-be-seen internal to and presupposed by the *logos*, on the other hand. If it is the case that speaking about life by letting it be seen in speech becomes impossible when life is in itself foreign to it, then this opposition is indeed so strong that it raises the question of the possibility of putting these two terms into relation. The method is useless when the *logos* residing in it borrows its light from the phenomenon about which it speaks. The method that lets something be seen runs up against an aporia when it must make the invisible visible. *How, then, is a philosophy of affectivity possible?*

The phenomenological method is constructed entirely on this aporia. Its first elaboration and formulation in the 1907 lectures shows the extraordinary work that enables Husserl to reestablish a connection between the phenomenological mode of treatment—elucidation—and that which it treats, namely, pure phenomenality and the origin of life. If, due to these aporia, this thematization progressively admits its powerlessness, this is because what the regard is directed toward can never stand before the regard. Its hold implies in fact a change of the object, the substitution of what is never an object by something which can become one. We have followed step by step the modalities and conditions of this substitution:

1. The dissolution of the *cogitatio* in the very process of clarification, under the "pure seeing" of the reduction;

2. The thematic turn, the replacement of the lost reality of the *cogitatio* with its general essence;

3. In other words, the replacement of immanence with transcendence;

4. The ontological and phenomenological promotion of transcendence as the law of being and the means of access to it, through the "extension" of the pure gaze beyond the "sphere of *cogitationes*";

5. The theory of the constitution of the transcendent essence in its perfect adequation to the "*logos*" of the method, that is to say, in the identity between them;

6. The ontological validation of the imaginary, of the particular "imagined" *cogitationes* that must serve as the basis for the aforementioned constitution, with the corresponding shaking of the founding distinctions of phenomenology;

7. The attempt to reduce the reality of the *cogitatio* to transcendence, understood as a "relating-to."

While the final or rather the two final observations were "critical," do not the first five theses establish the possibility of a theoretical knowledge of absolute subjectivity in spite of its immanence? What do we have to add to this?

To be sure, this foundation of the phenomenological method on the basis of its essential inadequation to what it is supposed to show remains unthought by Husserl and stands in complete opposition to the explicit presupposition of the doctrine that Husserl expresses as follows: "Descartes asked, as you will recall, after he had established the evidence of the *cogitatio* (or rather, in a phrase we have not adopted, the '*cogito ergo sum*'): What is it that assures me of this basic givenness? The answer: clear and distinct perception [*clara et distincta perceptio*]" (Hua II 49/37). Because, instead of giving itself to evidence, the *cogitatio* slips away from it, Husserl is forced to rework his problem from its first steps, by replacing the supposed "absolute givenness" of transcendental life with the long list of its objective equivalents and the complicated process of theoretically justifying them. It is as if there were some force pushing phenomenological thought from behind and guiding it, in spite of itself, along its strange path. The obstinacy to build rock by a rock a coherent methodological edifice on the ruins of the initial presupposition is the most striking proof of our thesis. Does material phenomenology have any other task than to make present the hidden motivation that has guided the thinking of traditional phenomenology? Should not what historical phenomenology did spontaneously through some sort of divination be thematically grasped so that the radical self-understanding of phenomenology may be achieved?

This would be to miss entirely the sense of the present critique, which does not want to understand only the cause of the thematic shift but also its ultimate roots, that is, the original dimension of the phenomenality that traditional phenomenology never perceives. It is not foremost a matter of arriving at a complete knowledge of the Husserlian text but of delineating an essential lacuna within it. Only the recognition of this lacuna can allow this knowledge to appear. This lacuna became apparent from the very first citations of the text: "every intellectual experience, indeed every experience whatsoever, can be made into an object of pure seeing and apprehension, *while it is occurring*" (Hua II 31/24). Material phenomenology seeks this original mode in which experience occurs. Its object differs entirely from its method, even if this method has no other aim than to allow us to "know" this object.

It would be a huge illusion then to understand matters in the following way. In its pathetic immediacy, absolute transcendental life—this life that is ours for each one of us—slips away from the regard and thus from every possible knowing, from everything that we call knowledge, speech, and *logos*. The sole way to gain access to any notion of this subject would be to put it before the regard, without which this life would be inaccessible, through the use of a substitute, its objective representation, which is not something that is but that stands for it: the noematic essence. The noematic essence is really nothing but this "representative," the representation of the absolute life.

This representation, to be sure, is in a sense a presentation. We do indeed see the essence of life in the pure seeing of the eidetic intuition whose primal character Husserl established, that is, its ability to attain the thing "in person" and in its reality. But the reality of the transcendent essence of life is not the reality of life itself. The presentation of this essence is not the presentation of life. Quite the contrary, this essence is only the exposure of each one of the characteristics that make up the substance of life before the regard, in such a way that each one of its characteristics undergoes an important modification in this representation. It is indeed the same characteristic, for example, the "exclusion of every transcendence," "self-givenness as finding its phenomenological actuality not in transcendence but in transcendental affectivity," this "affectivity," and "pathos" as such. Each characteristic, however, is only the same nominally. Its concrete content is different each time, and consequently the possibility of this nominal unity becomes problematic.

In the representation of the noematic essence, "pathos" is a transcendent given about which we can reflect and reason. It is something that is shown through another power of indication than its own, namely, through the transcendence of eidetic intuition. There pathos is an external, indifferent, and nonsensible content, analogous to the Greek phenomenon that becomes a phenomenon in the light of exteriority. But in itself and in its own actual life, it is nothing of this sort. It can only adopt a visible appearance on the condition of setting aside its own reality; it thus only appears in an irreal form. In the noematic essence of the *cogitatio*, pathos is nothing but an empty signification. Though it is stripped of its own reality, this is actually its most essential phenomenological feature, namely, the fact that it itself carries out revelation. This holds both for itself and for everything else that is.

Two questions can be posed here which, truly speaking, are aporias: (1) What enables us to call pathos this *dead* noematic content, lacking the capacity of sensing itself, when pathos is nothing but this capacity for the immediate suffering of life? (2) How can the essential characteristic of life, this suffering, which becomes a phenomenon only in the actualization of its living affectivity, be proposed as a transcendent essence and in terms of a noematic characteristic of life?

This aporia constitutes the problem of representation in general and that of the representation of life in particular. In the idea of representation, two presuppositions are tied together. This first involves a presentation that is carried out as an arriving before, in such a way that this arrival in the light of an "outside" constitutes the presentation itself—manifestation. Representation belongs to Greek phenomenality and is expressed in this way. The second presupposition, which is usually implicit, is that the content presented in a representation is a content presented for the second time. It is the coming into being of a being that has already existed before in another way. The second presentation is thus not like the presentation of a plate which is passed and remains the same through its movement, so that, having taken it, one can "take it again." Quite the contrary, with its second presentation the content of the representation has undergone a radical change. It has lost its reality and is no longer there as the irreal double of a reality included in the first presentation but thereafter lost. The most remarkable feature of Husserlian phenomenology, as we have seen, is that it always refers to the intentional correlate—the noema—as an irreality. This position is all the more significant in that it is affirmed at the very time when the power of making something manifest tends to be joined with intentionality. When appearing is conferred to transcendence, and when the phenomenological presupposition is that being is founded on appearing, the transcendent being is marked by an essential irreality. This fact attests to the invincible power of an intuition of life.

Moreover, if the noematic correlate is irreal inasmuch as in its transcendence it is placed outside of life, this thesis would flow back into life and center all of reality in life. This claim would have an immense philosophical scope. Life is not said to be real as a particular reality, which in this way would constitute a specific ontological region. To the contrary, all possible reality, including the reality of nature, the cosmos, the other, the absolute and even God, only becomes actual by being situated in Life. But can this claim go without any clearly defined phenomenological basis?

So, the aporia of representation remains. In representation, the noematic irreality strips away the reality of the presented being. But where does this reality reside? What is it made of? How does its first "presentation" become a phenomenon? Why is the second presentation only the presentation of an irreality? How can one recognize the reality that this representation represents when it never presents this reality? Would one not already have to know life, to be in possession of the original reality so that one would then be able to know that this is indeed what is presented to us a second time and that this second presentation is really not life itself but its double? All of these questions, which haunt philosophy from its beginning, are actually only one question, which at the end of our analysis can be formulated as follows: *How can we acquire a pure seeing of the* cogitatio? *How is the phenomenological method possible?*

Husserl's superb but unthought solution to the problem of method only displaces the problem and leads us back to ultimate questions. If we are in its noematic presentation without any indication enabling us to know that this essence is that of the *cogitatio*, and if none of its real properties—the non-intentional, the immanent givenness—can be detected in what is offered to pure seeing as an ideal meaning, and if in the transcendence where they are shown, there is never anything like a life of pathos, should not this method be abandoned? Should not the rule of method be overthrown? For, one would never have any concept of life, if the primal knowledge of life were not already included in the seeing that is directed toward it.

This primal knowledge of life is living itself. It is taken in and through living, in the phenomenological actualization of its self-revelation in pathos. Since each real property of real mental processes is revealed originally to itself and thus carries the initial knowledge of what it is within itself, a regard is able to arise on the basis of this knowledge. This regard casts the content of this knowledge—immanence and pathos—before itself. They are determined according to the modality of this mental process so that they can be seen as the irreal features that comprise the noematic essence of this *cogitatio*. That is what the founding proposition of phenomenology signifies: "every intellectual experience, indeed every experience whatsoever, can be made into an object of pure seeing and apprehension, *while it is occurring*" (Hua II 31/24). "While it is occurring" refers to the original self-revelation of what can afterward be placed before the regard and be known by it. *Instead of pure seeing allowing the absent or lost reality of life to be known in terms of its noematic essence, it is the immanent revelation of life in the* cogitatio *which allows seeing to see and know everything about life, to the extent that life can be known.*

The phenomenological method is the self-justification of the transcendental life of absolute subjectivity in its self-objectification. Objectification must be understood here differently from the way this concept is understood in modern thought. Modern thought espouses the general and implicit presupposition that objectification creates phenomenality. The phenomenality of life is precisely not founded on the arrival in the visibility of an outside. Instead, the phenomenality of life has already been revealed in its immanent living, when the project of grasping it through "cognition," in the sight of a pure seeing or in a direct indication in order to list its features in a coherent totality, can take place. I can represent my life to myself, and this principle is a part of life. But this possibility must itself be made possible. Paradoxically, this possibility does not reside in representation but in what ultimately founds representation. It resides in the Archi-revelation of the life in which every lived experience "occurs," in such a way that "while" it is occurring, one may try to represent it to oneself on the basis of what is being experienced. The noematic content is nothing but the representation of what is experienced. It does not presuppose what is experienced as a fact on a higher level but as its inevitable phenomenological and ontological presupposition.

The thematic turn leads us astray. It is true that it clears the path of access to life in what we refer to as "cognition," that is, in seeing. But the transcendent essence of the *cogitatio* does not purely and simply take the place of the *cogitatio*. It must "exist" in the Archi-revelation of its invisible pathos, if its being can be offered, likewise, to seeing as an essence. It is not simply the case that the seen is derived from life; in addition, seeing itself is only a modality of life. Without the auto-affection of life, nothing would ever be seen.

In the representation of the transcendental life of absolute subjectivity, the derivation of the seen from life does not belong to the same order as the life of seeing. While the seeing that lives from eidetic intuition is an occurrence in the life of the phenomenologist, a fact of a higher level, Husserl has already established that the life on which the noematic essence of the *cogitatio* is founded—in perception, imagination, judgment, and so on—need only be imaginary. But, what is imagined here is still only something "derivative," that is, something whose possible being, its phenomenological and ontological structure, is in life. The substitute can only exist on the basis of that which it replaces.

In every method, there is indeed an inherent letting-be-seen, and at first glance, method is nothing but that. The self-justification of transcendental life as its own self-objectification is the *logos* of phenomenology. To believe that this *logos* is the original phenomenon or, at least, that it is of the same order as the original phenomenon, this is the illusion to which traditional phenomenology has succumbed. Without even knowing it, it thus adopted the most common prejudice of Western philosophy. This label "Western philosophy" may appear to be vague. By "Western philosophy," I mean that philosophy whose *logos* is the phenomenality of the world and whose *logos* is based on this phenomenality. When facing this philosophy which governs our ways of thinking, one may list the following problems, among others, with the procession of their pseudo-solutions:

1. There is the confusion of *logos* with the ek-static phenomenality into which every seeing and every possible making seen is thrown, which is disastrous in that the essence of phenomenality is reduced to this and thus hides its original phenomenalization in life. To this, one must add:

2. Because of this, the essence of *logos* itself is perverted, if it is true that the manifestation presupposed as letting something be shown—by letting something be shown in the noematic essence of the *cogitatio*—implies the "fulfillment" of the Archi-revelation of life, both in its seeing and in what it allows to be seen.

But what is true about the *logos* of method is true about every possible *logos*, for ordinary language as well as that of science. The philosophy of language must therefore be completely rewritten, insofar as speech is never exhausted by letting what it speaks about be seen in what it says. Or rather, to the extent that this type of "letting-be-seen" excludes every letting-be-seen from itself, it is no longer transcendence but immanence.

Every Word (*Parole*) is the speech (*parole*) of life. What is shown in this Word, what is made manifest, is life itself. Saying is the pathetic self-revelation of absolute subjectivity. It says itself. It is the pathetic determination whose self-revelation is in every form of life. What it speaks about is itself, about the determination it is. It does not say what it says on the basis of something else about which it speaks; it says this on its own basis. That is what it means for the Word of Life to let something be seen by showing what it says in what it is speaking about. "Letting be seen" is to reveal in the pathetic self-revelation of life, in the way in which all things arrive in us, prior to every conceivable seeing and outside of every possible world. "That in which it speaks" is its pathetic flesh, while "that about which it speaks" is this flesh. So the suffering of pain is "clear" inasmuch as it is "obscure," which is to say that it is revealed to itself in and through affectivity as painful.[8] *Language is the language of real life.*

It is in this sense that the *logos* can first be true and, in some way, always is true. This is not because it presupposes the ek-static discovery of beings in perception and always points back to it and because it carries within its letting something be shown the space of the world in which every seeing exists. Instead, this is because the original essence of the truth is life, and the *logos* is nothing but life. The Word (*le Verbe*) that comes into this world is not the Greek *logos*, coming into the world as such. What comes into the world slips away from it in advance—it is the hidden life. The Greek understanding of *logos*, which is founded on the truth of perception, runs throughout the Middle Ages and determines the entirety of Western thought. Thus Jacob Boehme interprets divine Wisdom, as the first objectification of the divine essence, to be identical with its first manifestation. In this way, he believes that he justifies the existence of the world on the basis of the existence of the absolute. As is well known, Jacob Boehme's intuitions guide German Idealism and thus modern thought in its seemingly most autonomous and innovative developments, such as the philosophy of language. These intuitions must be called into question again. If the essence of *logos* resides in life, language can no longer be compared to a murder, for example. According to the Hegelian view transmitted by Kojève to the Parisian "masters of thought" in recent decades, language would be the murder of a reality that is suppressed and retained in the ideal form of the word.[9] Instead, the original saying is the phenomenological plenitude of life in its unshakable positivity.

If the essence of *logos* resides in life, is not the object of phenomenology—this life—identical to the *logos* of its method, contrary to their radical dissociation, which the present study has put forward? What would the disappearance of the *cogitatio* before the regard of the pure gaze signify if not this dissociation? And why would the entire process of the thematic turn and the substitution of the *cogitatio* with its noematic essence take place, if not because, in its immanent phenomenalization, the former is irreducible to the *logos* that lets it be shown but from which it escapes?

But from what *logos* does the *cogitatio* escape? It escapes from the Greek *logos*, which lets something be shown, but it does not escape from the original *logos* of life, which is the *cogitatio* itself. In its original content, the *logos* is certainly identical to pure phenomenality and depends on it. It is the appearing in its act of appearing which leads to itself and which is the Way. Or, to put it otherwise, all appearing is a self-appearing in a radical sense. The ultimate identity between *logos* and the phenomenon could not, however, be thought formally. Only a material phenomenology can recognize the manner in which it reveals the nature of its Saying and thus the essence of the logos itself in the phenomenological materiality of pure phenomenality and in the how of its phenomenological actualization. It is no longer a matter, therefore, of detecting the presence of a shared essence either here or there but of entering into its internal nature. In being crushed against itself in the invincible implosion of its pathos, life is an Archi-revelation, and in this way, it is the Way that leads to it. The Truth and the Way are indissolubly connected.

Is not the reduction of *logos* to the phenomenon established in the same way and with the same "Greek" presupposition, if, as we ourselves have shown, the *phainomenon* is not a formal but likewise a "material" concept, referring to the concrete phenomenality of ek-static visibility? But, it is the concrete character of this phenomenalization, its claim to autonomy, to show itself by itself, which is the illusion here. The reciprocity of the *logos* and the phenomenon continually veils what constitutes their ultimate foundation and alone allows them to show themselves as an actual phenomenon and *logos*. This illusion was revealed to us in the analysis of the phenomenological method. From its first formulation, the phenomenological method slipped into an aporia because its principle, letting something be seen, and more basically, the principle of principles, letting something be shown in the evidence of pure seeing, came up against a radical setback, namely, its inability to allow what was supposed to be seen. The term *radical* means that this setback concerns it from the beginning; it concerns the principle, the seeing, which is never itself seen. Instead of either adjusting itself to become adequate to it or to be based on it, the *logos* is now foreign to the original phenomenon and allows it to escape. In this sense, the object and method of phenomenology are entirely opposed to one another.

Method can ultimately be understood in two senses. Each one of them, it is true, points back to appearing and presupposes it. The duality of appearing gives the concept of method the meaning which we commonly give to it and which it has in the Husserlian determination of its meaning. There it is both letting something be seen in pure seeing—a direct indication—and a Way. But the rootedness of the *logos* in the *phainomenon* offers no parallel to the Word of Life. The latter founds the former and makes it possible. It is only to be seen in living, on the basis of the pathos that is essentially unseen within it. This is why the concealment in which every truth exists is not a formal negation, hypostasized as a philosophical entity henceforth possessing an illusory autonomy, the phenomenality of the world. It is not the type of phenomenological nothingness that is called the unconscious. The object of phenomenology is the Archi-revelation of Life in its irreducible positivity.

Although the seeing of the method, knowledge, science, and the Greek *logos* carries the pathetic plenitude of life as its founding antiessence, this does not prevent it from ever being seen. Inasmuch as one is confined to seeing, wants to see, and is directed toward what one sees, one must substitute the invisible *cogitatio* that resides there with an objective equivalent. This substitute is the noematic essence that the method laboriously constitutes and that is its own necessary condition. Once having established the conditions for this substitution (guarding within itself "the carrying out of the *cogitatio*" for which it substitutes), must not the detour instinctively followed by Husserl and staked out by markers placed one after the other, awaken our suspicion, causing us to doubt phenomenology and its ability to proceed by "direct indication"? Or, if life remains in the invisible with the bitter fate of never attaining reality "in person," is this not the detour of every regard? Are not the indirect ways that must be taken, such as the thematic turn and representation, prescribed by the very nature of things, as long as these things are the things of life?

When for the first time men slowly advanced toward one another, carrying piles of dried skins, sacks of grain, or salt, they blinked their eyes. For, they had to see what one never sees: the work included in these products, that is, *the living work*. Lacking this invisible subjective praxis of the effort and work of each one, they put before their regard what they imagined to be the equivalents of this pain and toil. They represented the number of hours of work, whether it was hard or easy, skilled or not, and so forth. In short, as will later be said, they represented *the noematic essence of work*, that is, the specific essence of the *cogitatio* as a transcendent essence. All economic reality, which is the reality of the world in which we live, is thus only the collection of objective equivalents, either ideal or irreal, that human beings have always substituted for their life, to the extent that they must be able to evaluate it and to account for it.[10] The phenomenological method is not the impossible return to the self, doomed to perceive only the shadows of some sort of useless and powerless autism. The intelligence within its reasoning is the intelligence of the world.

3

Pathos-With

Reflections on Husserl's Fifth Cartesian Meditation

Husserl's analysis of the experience of the other in the fifth Cartesian meditation is guided by three presuppositions that will determine it altogether. The first presupposition is that there is an other for me only if I have an experience of the other, only if, in whatever form or manner, the other is given to me, such that I find the other in my own life and that, in some way, the other is in me. For, if it were otherwise, one could say about the other what Epicurus said about death, that is, I would never have any contact with it—or with them. To be sure, I at least have the idea of death, and this is what makes the claim of Epicurus contradictory. With respect to the other, I would not even have the idea of the other without any contact with the other. This first presupposition of the Husserlian analysis makes it clear that the other does and must necessarily enter into my experience. Husserl puts it the following way: "These experiences [experiences of the other] and their works are facts belonging to my phenomenological sphere" (Hua I 122/90).

How does the other enter into my experience? How is the other given to me? That is the question of phenomenology, because phenomenology does not interrogate objects but the mode of their givenness, "objects in their how." For Husserl the other is given to me in and through intentionality. To say that the other enters into my experience means that the other enters into this primordial Outside into which intentionality casts itself, into this place of light where intentionality reaches and sees all that it sees. That is the second presupposition of the Husserlian approach. This second presupposition applies to the problem of the experience of the other an absolutely general presupposition concerning every form of experience whatsoever, and for this reason, every being whatsoever as it is a being that is and must be capable of being experienced. Here is the statement of this general presupposition: "Imperturbably I must hold fast to the insight that every sense that any existent has or can have for me—in respect of its 'what' and its 'it exists and actually is'—is a sense in and arising from my intentional life" (Hua I 123/91). And here is its application to the experience of the other: "It is necessary to begin with a systematic explication of the overt and implicit intentionality in which the being of others for me becomes 'made' and explicated in respect of its rightful content—that is, its fulfillment-content" (Hua I 123/91–92). And on the same note, Husserl states, "We must discover *in what intentionalities*, syntheses, motivations, the sense 'other ego' becomes fashioned in me and, under the title, harmonious experience of someone else, becomes verified as existing and even as itself there in its own manner" (Hua I 122/90).

To the extent that the alter ego is given in and through intentionality, it is given as "existing" and as being "itself there," in such a way that this "itself" is not really the alter ego as it is in itself but something that stands for it, which must be apprehended *as* being it and receives the sense of being the alter ego without ever really being it. This is not the other but what is intended as the other; this is not the real other but the other in thought. This is the other-thought, the noema of the other, which is to say the other as a noema, the other reduced to the sense of being other, the other in the mode of the how, the *als*, a quasi-other. §43, which immediately follows the claim cited above, is titled "The noematic-ontic mode of givenness of the other as transcendental clue for the constitutional theory of the experience of someone else." It is transcendental because it defines the possibility of the experience of the other. This possibility resides in a constitution so that what is opened to us is constituted and apprehended as being what it is. And, if this pertains to existence itself, it is an existence reduced to the sense of being an existence.

One will reply that it is a question of the other and consequently of an existence that, not being mine, cannot be given in itself but can only be intended as existing and precisely as the existence of the other. This is not the case. It is not because it is applied to the problem of the experience of the other, to the existence and the quiddity of the other, that the presupposition of phenomenology from the outset casts off this existence and quiddity into a noematic irreality. It is due to this presupposition itself, inasmuch as it consists of intentionality. Let us recall the passage cited earlier: "every sense that any existent has or can have for me—in respect of its 'what' and its 'it exists and actually is'—is a sense in and arising from my intentional life" (Hua I 123/91). We have the overwhelming proof of the universal character of this presupposition in the fact that it does not only concern the being of the other but every possible being in general, including the being of the ego itself as it enters into the experience of the other.

Besides, Husserl only presented the problem of the other as a "special problem" in the beginning. The transcendental theory that constitutes the other is actually only one part of the transcendental theory of the objective world. And that is the case because it belongs to the sense of "nature," as an objective nature, to be perceptible and so to exist for the other in the same way as it does for me. In a way, the constitution of the plurality of egos as other egos who perceive the same world necessarily precedes the objectivity of the world and makes it possible. The secret homogeneity of the transcendental experience of the other and the objective world insofar as they are constitutive of one another is what ultimately authorizes them to be placed side by side. The other is what is first given to me in the constitution of objective nature; the other precedes and founds objective nature. But this precedence quickly appears to be illusory and is overturned, if one notes that, if not the objective world, at least something like a world has already been opened so that this prior domain in which the ego is opened to the other may be accessed and experienced. It is indeed in a primordial world and thus within a world that the other appears. Additionally, this means that the other, even in its most archaic form, is necessarily given to an intentionality.

We have just formulated the third presupposition of Husserlian analysis. It involves the universalization of the second one, the presupposition of intentional givenness. That is to say, this latter presupposition is disassembled and flattened onto the former one by asserting that the necessary inscription of the other within my own experience is a noematic appearing as an intentional correlate. To say that the other is necessarily given in me means that the other is outside of me, as something transcendent. In this third presupposition, intentional givenness overlays givenness in my own experience; this is the central but unthought presupposition of the entire Husserlian analysis of the other and perhaps of his philosophy in general.

For a moment, let us place ourselves outside of this presupposition and ask ourselves what the experience of the other is such as it is really experienced by each one of us within ourselves. It is a desire seeking out some sort of response or nonresponse, an emotion before the reciprocity of this desire, a feeling of presence or absence, solitude, love, hate, resentment, boredom, forgiveness, exaltation, sorrow, joy, or wonder. Those are the concrete modalities of our life as a life with the other, as a pathos-with, and as a sympathy underlying all its forms. What does Husserl's fifth Cartesian meditation have to say about all that? Not one word. Or rather, might one say that all of that would only be an empirical content that a philosophy situated on transcendental plane would not have to take account into account? But how could what makes an experience possible be foreign to its actual content and, moreover, to what always makes up this content? Possibility means reality. The transcendental possibility of experience is the original phenomenalizing of the phenomenality of the phenomenon. So, for every conceivable phenomenon, it is what completely determines its reality. How would it be possible for a nonaffective condition to be the condition for that which, in and by itself, is necessarily affective?

If the regard Husserl casts onto the experience of the other allows the essence of this experience to escape, it is not due to a mere case of distraction or a lack of perspicacity. What regard could be more perspicuous than his? This regard carves up the entirety of being through essential distinctions that are important findings for philosophy today, such as the distinction between acts that present and those that represent, the detailed analyses of different types of syntheses and protosyntheses, association, temporalization, and so on. Those massive findings surround the problem of the fifth Cartesian meditation, but the concrete substance of interpathetic life slips away from Husserl's well-armed regard, perhaps because it is an intentional regard or simply because it is a regard.

Let us place ourselves again within this regard. If the experience of the other is intentional, it is a matter of knowing what sorts of intentions give us access to the other. In order to delineate these, Husserl first attempts to put them out of play. From *my experience*, he eliminates the other ego as well as everything that is related to or would imply the other in any way whatever. What remains is "what is specifically peculiar to me as an ego [*Das mir als ego spezifisch Eigene*]" (Hua I 125/94). This is an attempt, Husserl continues, "to delimit, within my horizon of transcendental experience, what is peculiarly my own [*das Mir-Eigene*]" (Hua I 126/95). Despite the brevity of the two quotes we have just cited, we can already detect in them the extraordinary difficulties that will leave a mark on the entire Husserlian analysis.

If ownness is truly my own, something proper to the ego, then only the nature of the ego can dictate and define what is its own. Is ownness, as what is the ego's own, not the ego itself? This thesis was already rejected by Husserl in his initial analyses and will be staunchly rejected once again, insofar as, on his view, it leads to solipsism. In order to avoid solipsism, must there not also be within the ego itself, along with what is its own, the experience of the other? Husserl must therefore distinguish between the ego and what is its own, even if there is nothing to say about its ownness other than that it is the ego's own. In any case, the ego and what is its own are, at once, essentially connected for a definition of ownness and necessarily separated for the rejection of solipsism. This split between the Ego and what is its own should have become the theme of an explicit problem.

A second difficulty is introduced with the second claim cited earlier: "to delimit, within my horizon of transcendental experience, what is peculiarly my own [*das Mir-Eigene*]" (ibid.). It is already understood that the being of ownness must be apprehended and grasped within a horizon. This is necessarily the case, one might say, in a phenomenological elucidation that is carried out as a transcendental reflection in which everything is given to it within the horizon of its reflection. But to say that ownness is given to phenomenological reflection within the horizon of reflection is to leave the question open as to whether or not ownness itself is given in this kind of horizon. This uncertainty appears all the more threatening as it concerns the Ego itself in addition to its ownness. Both of these terms are tied together in the enigmatic expression "what is peculiarly my own as an ego" (*ce qui m'est propre à moi l'ego*), where one term must found the other one without however reducing the other term to itself. But one does not know either how it founds the other term or how it can, while founding it, not reduce the other term to itself.

However, in a paradoxical manner, the elucidation of the ego's ownness does not begin with this ownness but with the world. In §44, the insight that relaunches the analysis is that if, through abstraction, I separate everything that is alien to me from the horizon of my experience, then this horizon, this transcendental phenomenon of the world, subsists. It should then be described carefully in a new way that stems from this abstraction. I eliminate from my experience of the world everything that results from the reference to others, including everything that confers the characteristic of living beings to animals, everything that confers the characteristic of personhood to human beings, and everything that confers to objects and the surrounding world all of the determinations that are due to their mattering for someone. In this way, my sphere of ownness (*Eigenheitssphare*), with a "nature included in my ownness," emerges (Hua I 127/96). This nature is different from objective nature and includes within it my own living body (*Leib*), which is different from all other bodies. In this nature, which is reduced to ownness, others are things and I am the objective phenomenon, "the human," with its organism, soul, in short, a psychophysical unity. The spatiotemporal form, reduced in a corresponding way, subsists in this world, as does my life, which remains an experience of the "world" and thus the possibility of experiencing what is foreign to me.

Let us make an important remark here. It is on the basis of this sphere of ownness and the elements included within it that the experience of the other will be constituted. For these elements are all worldly elements. Their original status is deposed once it is no longer a question of the bodies of others but of my own body, my "I can," and my ego. They are deposed in the sense that appearing, which is the basis of their being and for the understanding of their being, is their appearing in this first world of ownness. Or to put it otherwise, they are always constituted realities.

§45 seems to hear our question in asking "how I, the human Ego reduced to what is my own and, as thus reduced, included in the similarly reduced world-phenomenon and, on the other hand, I as transcendental Ego are related to one another?" (Hua I 130/99). The sphere of my objective ego reduced to its ownness is referred to the transcendental Ego. This return to the transcendental Ego entails the displacement of the question of ownness, that is, of this objective sphere reduced to the Ego itself. Now the Ego, as transcendental, defines what is its own; its own being functions as the being of ownness. But, the key meaning of this displacement of the question of ownness is immediately lost, inasmuch as the transcendental Ego itself gives way to the process of its self-clarification, which rests on the process of its self-constitution, and which puts us always in the presence of constituted elements. Hence, the Ego's transcendental sphere of ownness, where what is proper to it must be found, has the same essential structure as the human ego reduced to what is its own was shown to have: the structure of a world.

Moreover, the model that will guide the self-explication of the transcendental Ego in the self-reflection that introduces the transcendental reduction is the perceptual experience of the object. §46 begins by recalling its general style. When an object stands out and is noticed by attention, the experience of it goes on through a continual process that makes its inherent determinations explicit by a series of identifying syntheses. "Let us apply this," the text says. *That is to say let us apply this model of the perceptual experience of the object to the transcendental Ego. Let us identify the structure of the external perception of the thing with that of the immediate self-revelation of absolute subjectivity, that is, the internal essence of life.* The transcendental Ego is discovered as given to it, or rather, Husserl notes, as always already given to it prior to the explicating grasp, and "with an open infinite horizon of still undiscovered internal features of my own" (Hua I 132/101). Instead of problematizing the givenness that precedes explication in a radical way and instead of asking, in particular, if this givenness first consists in the ek-stasis of a horizon that the grasp will only have to decipher, the text conducts two acts of violence. It affirms first that the revelation of the ego is obtained in this grasp and consequently in this horizon, in a process of self-clarification, and second that what is thus revealed as the being of the ego is also its own. Husserl puts it this way: "My own too is discovered by explication [*Explikation*] and gets its original sense by virtue thereof. It becomes uncovered originaliter when my experiencing-explicating regard is directed to myself, to my perceptually and even apodictically given 'I am' and its abiding identity with itself in the continuous unitary synthesis of original self-experience" (Hua I 132/102).

There are essential limitations tied to the self-explication of the transcendental Ego that is carried out on the model and even, we might say, through the mode of perception. These are not only due to this process of self-explication, which Husserl does not speak about, but they are also tied to the temporality of the ego. Even though it is given as a perception of my concrete ego, these limitations are such that "this explication is carried out largely in acts of consciousness that are not perceptions of the own-essential moments it discovers" (Hua I 133/102). Recollections and potentialities are involved here, such that the large part of the ego's being—perhaps also its ownness?—escapes from perception *stricto sensu*.[1] In place of the contents, which arrive as givens in and through this mode of self-explication, what appear with absolute evidence are the structural forms that govern the mode of fulfillment of the process of the ego's self-explication.

The problem turns away once again from this Ego, whose ownness—what makes it into an Ego—was just missed, in order to consider the intentional object. Although it may have undergone this radical reduction to ownness, the intentional object is inscribed as well in the fully concrete being of ownness. The problem of the experience of others thus appears in the form it will adopt in the Fifth Meditation. It is a matter of knowing how this intentional object, which belongs to me, can yet be more than "a point of intersection belonging to my constitutive synthesis" (Hua I 135/105). It is a matter of knowing how the other, in some respect, can be irreducible to my own being, really other than me, transcendent in relation to me.

One knows Husserl's response to this question as the expression of the weighty presuppositions that we quickly evoked above. In this complex response, let us recall a few points. The guiding thread that Husserl claims to follow is borrowed from the sense of the word "other," the other ego. "Alter," writes Husserl, "signifies alter ego" (Hua I 140/110). *I, the original Ego, am the one who knows originally what an Ego is, inasmuch as I am one myself and I only have the experience of the Ego in me, in this racial ipseity that gives me to myself as this Ego that I am, as an Ego, and as the sole Ego who can tell me what it is to be an Ego.* This original Ego gives its sense to the other in every experience of the other that I can have. Let us pick up again Husserl's analysis: "Alter means alter ego, and the ego which is implied there is myself" (ibid.) What immediately follows belies or rather completely changes the meaning that we just recognized, taking it outside of the original site from which it draws its justification as well as its true intelligibility. Husserl states: "And the ego involved here is I myself, constituted within my primordial ownness, and uniquely, as the psychophysical unity (the primordial man)" (ibid.). Although the transcendental Ego constitutes the other through its experience of the other, the ego really at work in this constitution, which makes it possible, the "functioning ego" as one might say, is a constituted ego. It is an ego appearing in my primordial sphere of ownness and, in particular, inhabiting my body and making it an organism in this sphere and in this world. This is a paradoxical situation in which the sense of the other as an ego is constituted by my ego, while the constituted ego can only possess its true sense as my own ego through an original Ego that bestows it with this sense. The reason for this paradox, we say, will be shown to us right away in what truly will be the core of Husserl's explication of the experience of the other.

The other enters into my experience as a body appearing in the sphere of ownness pertaining to my primordial nature. The other is perceived within my ownness with the meaning of being an organism, which is to say a body inhabited by a constituted ego. Given that in this primordial nature only my body can, according to Husserl, be constituted as an organism in an original way, this other body is only capable of being given as an organism as well, inhabited likewise by an ego, as the result of an apperceptive transfer. This transfer starts from my own body, which transports this sense of being an organism from my own body to the other's body, which is henceforth perceived in the same way. This resemblance reconnects this other body to mine in the primordial sphere and allows my body to be conceived by analogy as another organism, as the body of an other.

Let us raise here for the first time the circle in which the Husserlian analysis moves, inasmuch as it presupposes what it attempts to explain. For, it is only because the other body is perceived as an organism—without me knowing why since I do not live in it—it is only because this perception of the other as a psychic body is presupposed that the necessary apperceptive transfer that will confer this sense of being an organism like mine through resemblance and analogy can be deduced.

Let us remain content for the time being to observe the way in which this apperceptive transfer (*Übertragung*), which is also called an assimilating apperception (*eine gewisse verähnlichende Apperzeption*), functions. We encounter another one of the themes destined to cover over the failure of this explanation. The experience of the other, for Husserl, is neither as enigmatic nor as incomprehensible as we imagine it to be. Quite the contrary, one must recognize that what happens in this experience happens everywhere. For example, consider the assimilating apperception. It enters into the most ordinary and common perceptions of our daily world, insofar as every apperception of any object whatsoever implies an intentionality directed toward the sense of this object and pointing back to a "primal instituting" (*Urstiftung*) in which the object was constituted for the first time in an analogous way. This transfer of sense takes place in pairing. Pairing will play a remarkable role in the experience of the other, but it too will in no way be restricted to this experience. It is a general law of the experience of objects and, as Husserl says, "a universal phenomenon of the transcendental sphere (and of the parallel sphere of intentional psychology)" (Hua I 142/112). Pairing is one of the most basic forms of the passive synthesis of association in which two contents given in the unity of one consciousness appear as forming a pair, which is to say that they are overlain due to the constitution of a single objective sense. The work of this pairing association is thus to transpose one single sense onto the paired group and thus of "an apperception of each according to the sense of the other" (ibid.).

When this schema of pairing will be applied to the problem of the experience of the other, in order to account for it by making it banal and by stripping away its enigmatic character, it will literally be flattened onto this experience. With its ontological weight borrowed from the universe of perception, its categories are completely inappropriate and thus shatter, falsify, and completely distort it. If pairing is an association and a unity of resemblance between two objects that exchange their sense, what is required for it to function in the experience of the other as the principle of this experience? In the first place, it is necessary for the other to be an object, and in the second place, for I myself also to be one or to have become one.

Applying the general theory of pairing to the problem of the other, §51 claims: "In that case of association and apperception which particularly interests us . . . pairing first comes about when the other enters my field of perception" and is thus presented as the object of my perception (Hua I 143/113). As for me, the ego only enters into pairing and functions in it as the constituted, psychophysical ego in my sphere of ownness. It is thus an object as well, as Husserl goes on to state: "I, as the primordial psychophysical ego, am always prominent in my primordial field of perception. . . . In particular, my live body is always there and sensuously prominent; but, in addition to that and likewise with primordial originariness, it is equipped with the specific sense of an animate organism" (ibid.).

What we have said from the start of our commentary about the demotion of the original Ego to the rank of a psychophysical ego appearing in an objective form in the world of my sphere of belonging takes on its full sense here. For one sees clearly how this demotion of the transcendental Ego is the condition of the experience of the other such as Husserl understands it. The worldly ego in the primordial sphere of ownness functions as the pivot of the pairing association with the body of the other, which itself is an object. The body becomes an organism in and through this pairing.

This demotion of the original being of the Ego also entails the demotion of the body. The body is no longer the radically subjective and immanent "I can" that I am and that is identical to my ego. It is still less what originally turns it into a body in its pure corporeality, as ipseity originally turns the ego into an ego. Instead, it is precisely a constituted body inherent to the sphere of ownness. *It is shown in ownness but not in itself.* Husserl observes that "my body is always there and sensuously prominent," while the original body is this sensibility itself to which both the constituted body and the reduced world of the sphere of ownness are present (ibid.). The typical paralogism and naivety of theories of the body is to say that to be given as my body, and so as an important element of what is my own, is to be given as a body constituted in and through my sensibility. That is to say, it refers to and presupposes sensibility, while this givenness presupposes an original body that is always the ultimate givenness.[2]

To the extent that the ego and the body, which work together to make the experience of the other possible, are a constituted ego and body, this experience is totally falsified. For, as Husserl said at the beginning of the Fifth Cartesian Meditation, the concrete and real experience of the other is a transcendental fact belonging to my phenomenological sphere. The transcendental Ego and my original body as the "I can" make and are this experience, while Husserl replaces them with the representation of two bodies paired in a world, in the world of my primordial sphere of ownness, which is not the primordial world but rather its self-objectification. If my original body experiences the other—not my body for my sensibility but my sensibility itself: this body outside representation and for this reason to which representation can open—this body can only be the represented and perceived body that is paired to the represented and perceived body of the other. When two bodies are grasped through a representative pairing, as can happen in some phases of the erotic process, such a situation, instead of founding an experience of the other and defining it originally, presupposes this experience instead. When the project of rejoining the other follows whatever paths it can, it is because desire and the other are already there.

The Husserlian analysis of the experience of the other, it is true, does not consist of a mere application of the schema of associative pairing borrowed from the world of perception. With this application, three problems emerge that convey the *sui generis* nature of this experience of the other. In contrast with what occurs in perception, first the object, which serves as the bearer of a sense originally created for it, namely, the sense of being an organism, will be transferred to a second object, the body of the other. This supporting object for the transferred sense is always there; it is my body that is constantly present to my sensibility. Second, the object onto which sense is transferred is never there and never given in itself. It is not presented but only represented or appresented; it is the other. This is the difference between perceptual experience and the experience of the other. In perceptual experience, the other side of the object can always become the front, while in the experience of the other the other side of the other's body appearing as an object in my sphere of ownness is the real subjectivity of this organic body. It cannot become present. Third, this is the motive for the difficulty perceived and addressed by Husserl: "How does it happen that . . . the transferred sense is appropriated with existence-status, as a set of 'psychic' determinations existing in combination with that body over there, even though they can never show themselves as themselves in the domain of originality, belonging to the primordial sphere (which alone is available)?" (Hua I 143/114). From this, Husserl's solution is as follows. Although the other is never given in itself, the apprehension of his psyche to his body, which is presented as an object in my sphere of ownness (an appresentation resulting from the associative transfer of sense from my organic body to the other's), gives me, as co-given and represented, the other's psyche at the same time as perception gives me this body. In other words, the other ego is given to me in a series of appresentations that "owe their existence-value to their motivational connection with the changing presentations proper, within my ownness, that continually appertain to them" (Hua I 144/114).

Let us reflect on these three points, which distinguish the specific experience of the other from ordinary perceptual experience. With regard to the first point concerning the constant presence of my body to my sensibility in my sphere of ownness, we have sufficiently shown that it is a derived and constituted phenomenon and not the original presence of the body to itself in pure corporeality, of the transcendental Ego to itself, outside of the world and constitution. Only this radically immanent presence defines a true constancy. It is the constancy of the transcendental life independent from every act of apprehension as well as from the site in which this type of act would be performed, while the presence of my body to my sensibility within the sphere of belonging has nothing that requires or implies its constancy. As a result, Husserl's argument is undone.

The second point is the most imposing. It holds that the experience in which the other experiences what is the other's own—in which the other's ego is given to itself and the other's body is given to its sensibility—forever escapes my direct perception. Husserl's entire analysis—the opposition between presentation and appresentation—is organized around this important fact, which seems to be undeniable, such that it grants credibility to the whole fifth meditation. But this important and undeniable fact is ultimately ambiguous. It covers two totally different meanings that must be clearly distinguished. Here is the one Husserl retains: the impossibility for me to directly access the subjectivity of the other is due to what is to be the other, and thus the experience of what is the other's own is given only to the other alone. That is why in my sphere of ownness, I can perceive only intentionally the body-object of the other. The fact that it is the body of the other, inhabited internally by the other's subjectivity, sensed and moved by it, is only an appresented sense.

Here is the second meaning of the impossibility to perceive intentionally the other in itself, which remains unthought by Husserl: this impossibility does not primarily result from what it is to be other but from what it is to be an ego, an absolute subjectivity. That is because every subjectivity understood in its original way, whether it is the other's subjectivity or my own, escapes in principle from intentionality, be it thematic or nonthematic, active or passive, and consequently, escapes from every perceptual presentation as well. Or to put it otherwise, it is not because the alter ego is an alter; it is because the other is an ego that I cannot perceive the other in itself. Or even more explicitly, it is because the transcendental life, as living, does not allow the hollowing out of the least separation that every intentionality, which exists in this separation, is deprived in principle of the ability to ever provide access to this life. And it is because this situation concerns my ego as well as the other's ego that we have challenged from the outset the Husserlian approach, which consistently replaces the original ego—which is never itself attained intentionally but only impressionally— with phenomena that are the products of its self-constitution or its self-explication, in particular, in the sphere of ownness where ownness dissolves entirely into a constituted being.

The third point of the Husserlian analysis reveals its paradoxical nature to us. Since the alter ego can never be perceived in itself but only appresented with its perceived body in my sphere of ownness, Husserl said that the existential value of this appresentation can only come from its constant tie with perceptual presentations, those of experience the real being of the other leads back immediately to this very same perception, which is to say to the perception of the body-object of the other, as the sole way to remove the obstacle. In what pertains to the question of the knowledge of the other and thus of a subjectivity, it is still to replace this with the mode of approach that is suitable for a thing, namely, perception, which is by nature the external perception of an object. Thus the living and pathetic intersubjectivity in which I am with the other, intersubjectivity in the first person, has given way to the experience of a thing, a dead thing whose "psychic" quality is only an irreal meaning associated with the being of a thing.

And yet, the style of this experience happens to be that of perception, and the other, like every perceived object, is ontologically reduced to its body displayed in my sphere of ownness. The other is given in the manner of this body object, that is to say, in a perceptual experience whose temporality points back to new intentional horizons destined to be filled intuitively in new perceptions. The other is not what it already is and forever will be for me outside of representation; instead, the other entrusts its being to representation and awaits to be confirmed, verified, corrected, or even possibly crossed out by it. Husserl states: "Regarding the experience of someone else, it is clear that its fulfillingly verifying continuation can ensue only by means of a new appresentations that proceed in a synthetically harmonious fashion" (Hua I 144/114). But these series of synthetically harmonious appresentations only exist insofar as the presentations with which they are connected and on which they rest are synthetically harmonious. The laws of perceptual presentations, therefore, regulate the unfolding and development of concrete pathetic intersubjectivity and not the laws of the pathos of these subjectivities in their internal co-belonging at the basis of life. For Husserl, the principle and model of our access to being, whether it is a question of our own ego or that of the other, is not the laws of desire and accomplishment, of suffering and enjoyment, of feeling and resentment, of love and hate, but once again, the laws of perception. In what is its ownmost (and, I would add, its most horrendous), it is a phenomenology of perception applied to the other.

What, then, could one say about an experience of the other in which perception would play no role at all? As an example, let us consider a concrete community, the one formed by the admirers of Kandinsky. Let us suppose that the members of this community never met and do not know one another. This may either be due to their small number or the free fantasy through which the eidetic analysis is developed. One will say that if these egos are together, although they have never been objects of perception for one another, there is nonetheless something objective that unites them, namely, the work that they admire. But for Kandinsky, the site of the work of art is not objective. The universe of painting is not the universe of the visible, if the being of each color is only in reality its impression in us and if the being of each plastic form is the invisible force that it traces, namely, the radically subjective and radically immanent "I can" of the original body, which is this impression and this pure force. Where the ego stands, there too stands its being with the other. What is shared in common, outside of representation and time and so permitting a community outside of representation and time, is the pathos of the work. This is at the same time the pathos of Kandinsky who creates it and of all those who "admire" it, which is to say those who have become this pathos.

Let us consider another community that is vaster and thus judged to be more significant: the community with the dead. To say that this community carries within itself the traces, in memory, of its absent perceptual support would apply only to the dead whom we have known but not to all of the others who are the humanity in us. As for the dead whom we have known, if perception constituted the key element of our common being with them, would this common being not disappear with perception itself or at least only remain as an object of representation, memory, and not as this pathos within us that is concealed from our acts of thought and secretly determines them?

But this becomes more and more troubling. If we reflect on this, the dead in our life cannot be identified with those who have departed from this world. Many still live whom we could revisit and thus see again, so that this visit would change nothing in us about their death, except to make it more apparent. Thus one must say that the life and death of the other, being in common or its interruption, in no way belongs to perception, neither to its factual possibility or impossibility. One might even think that the impossibility to perceive would be the condition for being in common. Kierkegaard goes so far as to say that being in common with Christ—what he calls "contemporaneousness"—is more difficult for those who would see Christ than those who do not. That is one feature of what he calls "the strange acoustics of the spiritual world," which holds that the laws of being in common are not in fact those belonging to things and the laws of perception. Here (*hic*) and there (*illic*) with respect to my relation to the other in the originally pathetic intersubjectivity in which I am with the other have nothing to do with the *hic* and *illic* spoken about in the fifth Cartesian meditation, where they refer to the *hic* and *illic* of bodies perceived in the primordial sphere of ownness.

This spiritual acoustics, which defies the laws of perception, defines our concrete relation to the other. The work of Kafka, for example, rests on this, as does Rilke's observation that it is among wives of alcoholics that one stands furthest from one another. If the modern world eliminates every form of community with the dead as much as it can—this community that played such a large role in past societies—if it detests even the idea of this, to the point of wanting, according to Nadezhda Mandelstam, to even suppress the mere mention of it, if it throws itself into what is there right before it at each instant, is this not because—as a world of science, technology and the media—it has pushed objectivity to the point of madness? Is it not also because being in common with the dead resides in this radically immanent, nonworldly, and pathetic subjectivity that we are?

This does not only pertain to the obscure and problematic concept of being in common with the dead or a god, but also to every possible being in common. It is always first and foremost carried out in us as an immediate modification of absolute subjectivity, as an actual and concrete being in common: the mother with the infant, the hypnotist with the hypnotized, the lover with the beloved, the analyst with the patient, and so on. Before intentionally grasping the other as other and before the perception of the other's body, every experience of the other in the sense of a real being with the other occurs in us as an affect. It is not a noematic or noetic mode of presentation that founds the access to the other; instead, it is a givenness consisting of transcendental affectivity and thus of life itself. The universal *a priori* of the experience of the other in its original modalities is located in the essence of life, not in intentionality and constitution. When perception enters into this experience and seems to play the leading role—for example, when we want to see someone or when lovers look at one another, undress, and touch—the question is precisely to know in such a case whether perception is what gives or does not give the other to us. Being in common, as desire, would have really preceded this perception, while perception, unable to respond to it, would send it back to itself, which is to say to the pathetic history of pure subjectivity and its own fate.

The impossibility of intentionality and perception, in particular, to attain the other's real being is not merely the central yet unclarified claim in the fifth meditation; it strikes at the heart of all the pseudo-solutions that are sought from this perception. Before concluding, let us clarify the nature of the failure that every noematic presentation of the other runs up against.

This failure is in fact twofold. First of all, it is the reduction of the other's real being in me to a noematic presentation outside of me, in the sense that allows the thing perceived by me to be another ego. The other ego is no longer a wound in me or the thrill of a real modification of my transcendental life; it is only an irreality, the correlate of an intentional aim. Husserl recognized this reduction of the experience of the other to the irreal, all the while trying to minimize it. If an abyss separates the real experiences of monads, the intentional community crosses this abyss and grants the object in the primordial sphere the sense of being another ego. This community, Husserl recognizes, is not nothing: "On the other hand, this original communion is not just nothing. Whereas, really inherently, each monad is an absolutely separate unity, the 'irreal' intentional reaching of the other into my primordiality is not irreal in the sense of being dreamt into it or being present to consciousness after the fashion of a mere phantasy. Something that exists is in intentional communion with something else that exists" (Hua I 157/129).

From this, the second and most serious aspect of the failure of the Husserlian view follows. If an abyss separates the real monads, the intentional communication crossing this abyss first involves replacing these real monads with their spheres of ownness. It is only within the sphere of ownness, in a first outside, that intentionality can function. But the spheres of ownness belonging to these monads are naturally just as separate as the monads themselves. They are even more so in that, reduced to its sphere of ownness and to what is its own, each "monad" is in fact removed from what is its ownmost, namely, its own pathos and the movement of life in it, which, as drive and desire, already propels it toward the other.

Let us note that the introduction of the very term monad into the text, with its Leibnizian connotation, results from the original definition of the

Ego in terms of intentionality, *which is ultimately to say, from a metaphysics of representation*. It authorizes the slippage of the Ego's immanent life into the world opened up by intentionality. The metaphysics of representation determines the ambiguity of the concept of ownness. This ambiguity surfaces and becomes explicit in §52 where Husserl says that, in order to distinguish myself from the stranger, "whatever can become presented, and evidently verified, originally—is something I am" (Hua I 144/114).

§55 makes clear the radical separation between the spheres of ownness, the sophism that is used in an attempt to overcome this separation. The issue is to understand how the other's body *illic* in my sphere of ownness and this same body *hic* for the other in the other's own sphere are nonetheless the same, or to put it another way, how these two spheres can be identified in and through the identification of this body. Husserl writes: "But the enigma appears only if the two original spheres have already been distinguished—a distinction that already presupposes that the experience of someone else has already done its work" (Hua I 150/121). Yet, the entire analysis in the Fifth Meditation presupposes these two spheres of ownness. It presupposes that the experience of the other has done its work, that there is an other with another sphere of ownness, and that the body *illic* of my sphere of ownness is the other's body *hic*. This is what makes pairing, association, and analogy possible in my sphere of ownness. But, all of this can be found only because the analysis presupposes it beyond this sphere of ownness. Perception never founds this presupposition but always presupposes it. This presupposition has its roots in the transcendental life where the ego arises and can be understood only by starting from the basis of transcendental life.

The drive is rooted in life and in it alone, insofar as the drive is originally nothing other than the pure subjectivity of this life. The drive is the experience life has of itself, supporting itself and carrying its own weight even to the point where this weight becomes unbearable. To unload this all too heavy weight, to attempt to deliver oneself from its malaise or suffering, these movements are born in the life of its own essence. They are the movement of the drive. Since life continually affects itself without being able in any way to put itself at a distance or to escape itself, and since it is the greatest danger to itself, it enters into the drive and attempts in one way or another to master the drive.

The Fifth Cartesian Meditation's paralogism consists of describing the experience of the other on the basis of the objective perception of the other's body. It gives this intentional constitution to explain this experience, while it really should be a matter of explaining the ultimate cause of this constitution and thus of grasping its own possibility. One might say that phenomenology mistrusts ultimate explanations and is attached primarily to problems of description. But a description that allows the "thing itself"—the pathos of every concrete intersubjectivity—to escape as it occurs cannot be justified, even on the level of facticity.

One will still say that there are many other Husserlian texts on the problem of intersubjectivity, including the unpublished manuscripts collected in the three volumes of the *Husserliana* devoted to this problem. Among them, one can follow the lead of Didier Franck and highlight those that promote the drive and sexuality as fundamental forms of the relation to others.[3] A drive-based conception of community is thereby suggested. But the drive is introduced there outside of its appropriate theoretical context. Moreover, it is immediately interpreted and thus taken to be self-evident that the essence of the drive is intentional. Due to the confusion of life's immanent movement with an ek-static projection, the movement of life is torn from its original site and is simply destroyed. Instead of being able to pose the question of intersubjectivity on a truly new basis, these manuscripts only reinscribe phenomena in the traditional domain of the subject-object relation—including, intuition, its fulfillment, and more broadly, noetic-noematic analysis—whose main sense and philosophical power are precisely to keep us from departing from the subject-object relation.

The critique of the fifth meditation sketched here is in no way a critique of phenomenology. Quite the contrary, all of the questions that we have posed to the Husserlian text are phenomenological questions. They lead back ultimately to one sole question, the phenomenological question evoked at the beginning: *How* are things given to us? The object of phenomenology is this how as such. By responding to the problem of knowing how the other is given to us through the thesis of intentionality and by repeating, with respect to the other and intersubjectivity, the presupposition that intentional phenomenology is the universal *a priori*, the Fifth Cartesian Meditation calls us to revisit this presupposition as a result of the difficulties that it raises. This is not simply Husserl's presupposition, but also that of all the phenomenology that developed afterward. It invites us to nothing less than a rethinking of phenomenology and its ultimate phenomenological foundation.

For a Phenomenology of Community

The idea of community presupposes the idea of something in common as well as the idea of community members who have in common what is held in common. The idea of community thus puts four questions before us:

1. What is this reality that is held in common?
2. Who are the ones who have this reality in common?
3. How do the members of community have a share in what is common to them? To put it another way, what is the mode of access by which and due to which they enter into possession of the common reality?
4. Or, how is the common reality given to them, to each one of the members of the community?

The last two questions attest to the phenomenological character of our investigation. For, as is well known, phenomenology does not deal with things but their givenness and the mode in which they are offered to us. It does not deal with objects but, as Husserl says, "objects in their how."

We want to clarify the enigmatic being of community. Our first analysis had the sole effect of multiplying the difficulties, making four questions emerge where there was only one. Perhaps these four questions are only one, that is to say, the reality that is held in common, the reality of the members of the community, the reality of the how by which they have access to the common essence, and the reality of the how by which this essence is given to them. Perhaps there is only one and the same reality, one and the same essence, of the community and its members. Let us give a name right away to this single and essential reality of the community and its members: life. So, we can already say that the essence of community is life; every community is a community of living beings.

If it is true that phenomenology does not deal with things but the how of their givenness and thus with pure manifestation as such, this is because the life about which we are speaking is not a thing, a being of a certain kind, given with a set of properties and functions such as mobility, nutrition, excretion, and so on. Life is a how, both a mode of revelation and revelation itself. This is why the order of our four questions should be reversed or, if you will, their identity is only now perceived.

The question is how what is held in common is given to the members of the community. The fact that this question—the fourth one—comes first means that what the members of the community have in common is not a something, this or that, such as a patch of land or a job. Instead, they have in common the way in which these things are given to them. How are they given to them? They are given in and through life. But, our question must then be reformulated: How are things given in and through life? How is life given?

Life is given in its own way, in a completely unique way, even though this singular mode of givenness is universal. Life is given in such a way that what it gives is given to itself and that what it gives to itself is never separated from it, not in the least. In this way, what life gives is itself. Life is self-givenness in a radical and rigorous sense, in the sense that it is both life that gives and life that is given. Because it is life that gives, we can only have a share of this gift in life. Because life is what is given in this gift, we can only have access to life in life. No road leads to life except life itself. In life, no road leads outside of itself. By this, we mean that it does not allow what is living to cease living. Life is absolute subjectivity inasmuch as it experiences itself and is nothing other than that experience. It is the pure fact of experiencing itself immediately and without any distance. This is what constitutes the essence of every possible community. Again, what is shared in common is not some thing; instead, it is this original givenness as self-givenness. It is the internal experience that brings to life everything that is and makes what is alive in this experience become alive in and through it alone.

In a community, there is not only life but also the members of the community.

Who are they? Where do they come from? What are they supposed to do there? What does this proliferation of the living in life signify? Are we able to have any sort of answer at all to questions of this kind? We do know, however, that nothing can enter into life except through life. With respect to its essence, the members of the community are thus not something extrinsic, a mere addition, or the effect of odd or empirical circumstances. They are not empirical elements that, put together by chance, would suddenly form a community. Only the living—absolute subjectivities—enter into the community of life. But, they enter into this community on the basis of the life within them. Once again, we must begin from life if we hope to understand what we want to understand about the bare existence of the living.

Life is the experience of itself. Once this experience occurs, it is singular in a radical sense. It is necessarily this experience, irreducible to any other experience. For example, each anxiety is this anxiety. By touching each point of its being in the immediacy of its auto-affection, it fills everything. It fills the whole world, as one says figuratively, even though it is not in the world. It is only the whole of being, insofar as it is not in any world and insofar as no horizon overflows it from any side. It leaves no room to escape where there would be license to get rid of oneself and where there would be something else besides oneself.

As for the internal structure of life due to which life is each time a living being, Kafka expresses this in the following way: "It is a matter of chance that the ground on which you stand cannot be any larger than the two feet that cover it." Whether it is a question of "chance" or the unbearable weight of life driven back to itself, the radical interiority of life—an interiority in which life is adjusted point by point to itself—is constructed from within. This experience is not what it is in the external identity of the thing we refer to as the "same"; instead, it is what it is as an experience adjusted point by point to itself, by feeling and experiencing itself in this way. In other words, the essence of absolute subjectivity as the pure fact of immediately experiencing oneself is likewise the essence of ipseity.

The essence of ipseity is not an ideal essence or the correlate of an eidetic intuition. It is only this way in our representation and in irreality. But, as a real essence that is actual and living, it is each time an actual self. It is the identity between the affecting and the affected in an auto-affection that radically individualizes and puts the stamp of individuality on everything that is auto-affected. Subjectivity is the *principium individuationis*. Subjectivity gives birth necessarily, each time to an ego, an individual in the transcendental sense, in the sense of what can and must be transcendental. To the extent that the subjectivity of life constitutes the essence of community, the subjectivity of life is precisely a community, not only of life but also of a potential group of the living.

The community is nothing but this group of living individuals. The concept of the individual in the sense that we have highlighted here is so essential that there can only be a community with it. The attempt to oppose the community and the individual—to establish a hierarchical relation between them—is pure nonsense. It amounts to opposing the essence of life with something that is necessarily entailed by it. When one political system or another advocates if not the elimination of the individual at least its subordination to more essential structures or totalities, even a greater community than it, this is not a community. The totality, for example, of a bureaucracy is an abstraction, which has taken the place of life and claims to speak and to act in its name. In life the individual is never an unnecessary excess or a subordinate; instead, it is the proper mode of phenomenological actualization of this life. The situation in which the lowering of the individual occurs is not only a current event and politics; it is also theoretical and thus claims to be universal. It occurs everywhere in one way or another. For example, in the world of modern technology, objectivity is given as the site of every conceivable truth, while life and the individual, which are consubstantial, are eliminated. Whether it knows it or not, whether it wants it or not, the slogan of this theoretical objectivism rejoins the slogan that was formulated more clearly on the political level: "Long live death!"

If the fate of the individual and the community are linked in such a way that they share the same fate, then it is important to clarify the status of the individual in a way that is freed from misunderstanding. Let us reflect again on the word that revealed this status to us. If the ground where I stand is never any larger than the two feet that cover it, their contact is absolute subjectivity. This point of contact defines an absolute Here (*Hic*), the here (*Hic*) where I stand, where I am, or more precisely, that I am. This *Hic* is the ipseity of subjectivity. What characterizes this Here (*Hic*) is: (1) it can never be seen because in the ipseity of subjectivity—that is, in subjectivity—there is no distance; there is not the least separation into which a regard might slip; (2) never seen, it cannot be seen in any way, no more in a there, a There (*Illic*) of any kind, than in a supposed *hic* that would be able to be changed into this there (*illic*). The absolute Here (*Hic*) is undeclinable, and nothing can ever trade places with it; (3) it is never seen because it is never in a world, because it is not shown in the ek-stasis of being, and because it is not a phenomenon in the phenomenological and Greek sense. In addition, the here (*hic*) escapes all of the categories belonging to and depending on this world, such as intentionality.

Here we must be careful. If we want to think community at the same time as the individuals and the egos that make it up, we must radically dismiss the way we typically understand the ego, including its here (*hic*), its body, and its many properties. We understand it precisely *as* an ego. We take it to be this ego, which is the way we understand it to be. That is to say, it comes into the world and the horizon of the world, and it shows itself there as being this ego, as yours and mine. In Husserlian phenomenology, every ego is constituted by an intention that gives it the sense of being an ego, more precisely, the sense of being my ego or your ego. Just like its being, the ipseity of this ego is reduced to the sense of being an ego, to showing itself as an ego, and to being perceived as an ego in this original world in which intentionality is deployed.

Now the greatest mystery is the question why intentionality perceives what is shown in the world as being an ego and gives it the sense of being an ego. For, the power that gives sense can only give the sense of being an ipseity to what is shown in the world, where no ipseity or ego is possible, if ipseity has already deployed its essence elsewhere. Intentionality rises only at dusk. To put it simply, at least when it is a question of the ipseity of the ego, intentionality always arrives late.

Let us insist that the little, the very little, that Western philosophy has had to say about the members of community has been borrowed blindly from this as-structure of the world. This becomes especially clear when this structure is brought to its truth in modern metaphysics, where it becomes the structure of representation. To represent is to present-as. In representation, the ipseity of the I is inscribed in the following way: I represent myself. That is to say, I present something as myself, as my ego or yours. But why is what is put before a me or a you? We know nothing about this. And what is this me or you? In representation we know nothing about this either.

In representation, it is true that the ego is duplicated in a strange way. It is not only the object of this representation but also its subject; it is not only what is presented but also what presents and what presents to itself. It represents itself. Again, one should take note that this ego—the true ego, the transcendental ego that accompanies every representation and to whom every representation is presented—is only thought in terms of representation. Ultimately, it is identical to representation and thus to the world for which representation is the last avatar. "I represent myself" expresses the structure of representation. If, in this expression of the structure of representation, the ego appears now as the pole of identity to which the represented is related, and if this pole of identity is invested with an ipseity, this would not even be a mere presupposition but rather only a careless use of language, if Kant is right that the "I am" is only a mere proposition. One cannot see what can motivate this proposition, since every attempt to say something more about this ego, to assign it any sort of being whatsoever, is a paralogism. Contemporary philosophy has directed a radical critique against the philosophy of the subject and the ego-subject. But, it has forgotten that the philosophy of the subject itself produces this critique, its own self-destructing. Hence, the contemporary critique is only an unconscious restatement of it. Now why would the ego-subject and its implicit ipseity decompose to the point of disappearing in representation and more generally in the light of a world, if not because the essence of ipseity is completely irreducible to this light and never shines in it and because it is not a Greek phenomenon?

Here we must give more attention to our own thesis, which we have perhaps too quickly accepted as being self-evident. We claimed that the essence of community is life and that every community is a community of the living. Inasmuch as life is immediately auto-affected without the separation of any difference, outside of representation and the world, inasmuch as ipseity is born in this nonworldly experience, inasmuch as the occurrence of this experience is a singular and determinate experience, then everything that has to do with the community, its members, and their relations, is from the outset taken outside of the world, even though the world would seem to be the place in which human beings are together. Must we then say that, in spite of all appearances, every community is invisible? Let us take this risk.

One comment, however, must be made. In order to clarify the being of community, we have made an appeal to phenomenology and its presuppositions. For phenomenology, the following formula holds: "so much appearance, so much being" (Hua I 133/103). But for phenomenology the appearance that founds being is the Greek phenomenon. It is what is shown and shines in the light. We have just radically rejected these presuppositions, if only to introduce the problem of community. By contrast, traditional phenomenology relied on these presuppositions in order to resolve this problem—which was up to then unsolved—for the first time and to do so with splendor. This problem is presented in terms of the problem of the experience of the other, and rightly so, if community cannot be reduced to its own essence or to its members but yet implies the relation maintained directly between them. In order to establish the relation to the other, one must distance oneself from the interiority of the *cogito*, which cast its shadow over the development of Western philosophy, as it does, one must recognize, over our own analysis as well. When the human being is no longer enclosed in itself in a pseudo-interiority as if it were in a box it cannot escape, and when the human being is understood as a being-in-the-world and thus as being among things and with others, the problem of the other is resolved. Or rather, it appears that it has only been a problem in the elaborate constructions of awkward speculations. *Dasein* is itself a *Mitsein*.

Max Scheler gave this phenomenology of what is undeniably there in the world a radical, systematic, grandiose, and heartfelt development, because it was ridden by the aporias that always torment this type of proof before it collapses. Scheler's thesis is shared by Husserl's Fifth Cartesian Meditation, with a slight difference, a tiny nuance, a little nudge through which he attempts to transform what was headed toward defeat into a definitive victory. For Husserl and Scheler (I will limit myself to the result, setting aside the problems due to time constraints), I perceive, I attain directly in my intentionality the psychophysical being of the other—the other's body—not as a thing analogous to other things but as a living body, which is inhabited by a psyche, a body that sees, takes, feels, suffers, experiences pleasure, and so forth. The living body or the psychophysical being of the other is a totality, an inseparable unity, because it is impossible to perceive one aspect of it—the bodily aspect—without perceiving the mental aspect, or vice versa.

What can be said, however, about these two aspects? Even if a pairing or an infinitely powerful association joins them inseparably, this does not prevent us from posing crucial ontological and phenomenological questions about them. One must ask: Are these two terms homogeneous facts of one single reality and one and the same stuff? Is it the power of givenness that gives them the same intentionality, or two different intentions? Is it a question of intentionality in both cases? Although these questions are formulated quickly and poorly, we can nonetheless establish that the answer to them is negative. The psyche of the other, the other's soul, is radically different from the other's body-object, and moreover, the psyche's mode of givenness is completely different from the body.

In the Husserlian analysis, this difference is recognized only then to be falsified and dodged as much as possible. This is how: while the body of the other is presented to me, that is to say, really given to my perception, which reaches it as what it is, the other's psyche is only appresented. It is given in pairing with my perception of the other's body, but the other's psyche is neither given nor perceived in itself. It is not presented but only represented. The difference between the perception of the other's body and that of the other's soul is the difference between the acts that give something in person and those that give only a representation of the thing but not the thing itself, that is, between a perception and an image, copy, or double. It is a difference between two types of intentionality; this difference is internal to intentional phenomenology and explicable by it. In the experience of the other, intentional phenomenology does not merely maintain but verifies its ultimate presupposition, whereby every sense that any being whatsoever can have for me—in respect of its essence or existence—is rooted in intentional life (Hua I 123/91).

Everything pertaining to the experience of the other and thus to community itself is reducible to and explicable by sense. I, who perceive myself here, perceive the other in my sphere of ownness as another body, as a living body, and thus as the body of the other as an alter ego, who is there and who from the other's there perceives me as a there that is a here for me. It is the same there, which is a here for me, which is a there for the other. Likewise, all objects form one and the same system of objects, which are seen in a way by me and in a way by the other, according to two systems of appearances that are comprehensible and explicable on the basis of one single system of objects and one single objective world. It is a community of those who perceive this one and the same objective world and who, as the systems of these different perceptions between them, are the different appearances of one and the same reality, one and the same world. The ideal reality of this objective world—concerning which systems of representation harmonize—is what human beings have in common. This is why we have called phenomenology a perception of sense and nonsense.

Let us raise one question, however. Why in the perception of the other's psychophysical body is only the body perceived, while the other's soul is only appresented, which is to say that it is not perceived and, Husserl adds, can never be? Would this be because it is the other, or for the more basic reason that what makes up the being of an ego, be it the other or myself—that is, the ipseity and absolute *haecceity* of the subjectivity of life—carries no outside within it, cannot be perceived in it, and escapes from every conceivable intentionality?

An abyss is hollowed out under the footsteps of intentional phenomenology. It is the imperceptibility of the ipseity of life that is the ultimate obstacle set before the regard of thought, but that thought can never see. Scheler believed that he could eliminate this abyss on the basis of an unheard of thesis, namely, that I perceive not only the body of the other but also the other's psyche. That is the nuance brought to the Husserlian analysis. I perceive not only the red of the other's face but also immediately and indissolubly the other's shame. The psychophysical unity is a primal unity, and it is only afterward that a distinction can be introduced between two series of phenomena that are, however, both placed under the heading of phenomena, as things that shine in the light where the intentional regard encounters them.

Scheler recognizes and affirms the condition for this perception *sensu stricto* of mental reality: the mental is a transcendent reality, the correlate of a possible intention. And in fact, the world is not first only physical or material; instead, it is a world constituted with axiological and affective predicates. It is a peaceful or threatening world, dangerous or advantageous; it is a mental world, full of fever, confrontation, resentment, boredom, and fatigue, a world populated with regards that look at me or flee me or simply ignore me. For Scheler, vortexes are formed in this anonymous mental flow. This means that these various psychic realities are not dispensed either by chance or indifferently; instead, they are organized according to various minisystems. They are traced back and related to centers that are the various egos for whom they are lived experiences.[4]

Thus, one must ask Scheler: why are these vortexes, which are egos, formed in this psychic current, and why is the unity of the psychophysical being divided into what is physical, which is to say, what does not feel anything and does not feel itself, and what is mental, which is to say, what does feel and experience itself? One must ask further: What is the essence of ipseity and what is the essence of life? Let us return then to our problem.

In life, the relation between living beings can only be understood on the basis of the essence of life, which is their essence. That is to say that this relation must be understood outside of the as-structure of the world, intentionality, and sense. We are conceiving this essence of life in terms of auto-affection. Auto-affection, we have shown, causes this life each time to be a life. We would call this an "ego," if that would not inevitably be understood as the ego of representation that is projected and emerges on the horizon of the world as the being that is an ego. If this transcendent ego, whether it transcends or is transcended, is absent from the relation between the living in life, then this relation would have nothing to do with what classical thought and phenomenology describe as the experience of the other. On their description, for such an experience to be the experience of the other, the other must be perceived as other, as other than myself, as the alter of my ego. As an ego, I am thus jointly implicated in this experience as myself, and I am in a certain way jointly perceived in this experience as being myself.

But this never really happens in the original experiences that we have of others, as long as we are really with them. That only happens insofar as the ego—be it the other's or mine—is an irreality, the correlate of intentionality and its noematic sense, it does not carry in itself the reality of life in the actualization of its auto-affection. If we consider, for example, the relation of the infant to its mother, at least in its first stages, precisely because it occurs outside of the world and representation, it does not imply either the emergence of an I as an I or an other as an other. The infant does not perceive itself as an infant any more than it perceives its mother as its mother. And that is because the horizon in which it could perceive itself to be its mother's infant has not yet been awakened. Every description that reports this apperception or implicitly presupposes it as the apperception of a relation through which the infant would understand itself, for example, as loving its mother, is a naïve description. It retrospectively projects the structures of representation onto a pure experience engulfed in its subjectivity, where there is not yet a world or any of the relations that would constitute it. As to this pure experience we ordinarily refer to as infancy, we can conceive it only in terms of the subjectivity we are talking about as driven back to itself, left to its own modalities, and unable to get rid either of them or itself. It suffers them in a primal suffering that defies every liberty and every possibility of getting rid of oneself in the ek-stasis of a world.

One will say that our example, as hackneyed as it may be today, is an extreme case. We have sought to conceive the human community outside of the world, as if it were not a community of human beings in the world, a community of human beings confronted with this world, in such a way that the different characters of concrete communities depend in fact on the different modes of this confrontation, on the relation to nature in work, and on working together. By setting aside this unavoidable situation, do we not place ourselves on the level of an abstraction? Would the phases of the formation of a human community, which is to say a social community, have only a genetic meaning? But does not genesis have only a historical scope that delineates a phase destined to be passed by? Or rather, is it the return to the *arche*, to the ever present and acting? Just like Nietzsche's animal, Freud's infant does not refer to a stage in a process; it is the hidden name of an essence, namely, the essence of life. This is why its characteristics are found in every stage of life, regardless of its age.

Let us consider another example: hypnosis. Whatever uncertainties may surround this strange phenomenon, the only certain thesis that one may formulate on this subject is the following: neither the hypnotist nor the hypnotic exists for the hypnotic. This is because neither one of them appears in a world or is a phenomenon in the Greek sense. To put it another way, the hypnotic does not represent either the other or him or herself, because the hypnotic is in life and in life there are no representations.

This situation probably occurs in animal hypnosis as well. When a squirrel is mesmerized by a snake that is prepared to swallow it, it does not perceive the snake as a threatening other—in the way in which one says that a cow perceives the grass as something good to eat—any more than it perceives itself as being in danger. As long as such a distinction would subsist, the fascination or the hypnosis would fail. It would seem that it can only be carried out when the "animal" coincides with a motion or a force within it, in such a way that it is nothing but this force and allows itself to be carried away by it.

One will object that this hypnotic situation is even more rare than that of the infant and that it would be paradoxical to conceive a community of adult human beings on this model. This would be true, unless every possible community were of the hypnotic order, including the most evolved communities in which the share of intelligence would seem to be the largest. So let us consider yet another example: the community formed in psychoanalysis between the analyst and the patient. Or rather let us consider this, for the analyst does not exist for the patient, at least as a representation; the analyst is withdrawn from the patient's regard and acts as if he or she were not there.

Psychoanalysis is a therapy that applies mainly, at least initially, to the neuroses of transference. This therapy consists precisely in a transfer, which is to say in the repetition of the transference it takes for therapy. It is thus illuminating in two ways, to the extent that it puts us in the presence of the essence of transference twice: the first time as it occurs in the life of the patient, and a second time as it is repeated on the couch of the analyst. In truth, it is incorrect to speak of two times. The transference does not happen just one time in the life of the sick patient; it happened and was continually repeated there; it was repetition. The repetition sought in analysis is a very specific type of repetition; it is a repetition that seeks to be the last and that aims to put an end to itself. But how?

To answer this question, wouldn't one first need to know why the transference was a repetition in life? It was repetition because it was in life, and because life is repetition. It is not repetition, as we commonly represent it to ourselves, as an event occurring a number of times in the world. Life is repetition inasmuch as it does not occur in a world. In the absence of every act of putting at a distance and in the impossibility of introducing a distance between life and repetition, life is forever what it is. That is also why it does what it does and continues to do so. In the radical immanence of the absolute subjectivity of life, which is to say in its nondifferentiation with itself, there resides the condition of the possibility and the essence of every action. This essence is nothing but the actualization of a force in its immanence to itself and is made possible by this force. That is why in both life and analysis, transference is repeated and repeats itself as a force. That is why it is an obstinate action (*Agieren*), immersed in itself, submerged by itself and unable to do anything but what it does. It is a sleepwalking and blind action, indifferent to everything around it, acting in a hypnotic state—"unconscious."

This can be called "unconscious," if consciousness means what is represented in a world and shown in its light, and if everything that belongs outside of this light and is unable to be illuminated by it, is found outside of experience. It is thus nothing, or at least, something that is never shown in itself and whose existence can only be inferred on the basis of something that is shown, indications such as the associations made by the patient.

But what is it that is repeated and acts in transference as a force? Would it be nothing that we know about, nothing conscious? Or, to the contrary, would it be consciousness in itself, which, unlike every represented being, cannot cease to be present, such as the affect, which Freud says is never unconscious? One should understand the pertinence here of Mikkel Borch-Jacobsen's observation, which affirms that in analytic transference the unconscious is shown in the nude, such as it is in itself.[5] This is why, we might add, psychoanalysis organized the repetition of this transference. In the end, even though psychoanalysis imagines that it can confide the matter to language and verbalization, the unconscious must be sought where it is and such as it is, namely, as this brute force and pure affect.

Why is force an affect? Why is the affect a force? In what way is the question of the primordial pair of force and affect our question? In what way is it the question of community? No force is possible or able to act, if it is not first in possession of itself, and if it does not experience itself in the immediacy of life, which expels every act of putting at a distance. The phenomenological actualization of this experience—this non-Greek phenomenality—is affectivity as something undeniable, irreducible, and absolute. This phenomenality is never excluded; it subsists when everything else is excluded. In accordance with Descartes' decisive insight, when the whole world is put out of play by supposing that it is perhaps only a dream, the fear experienced in this dream is nonetheless absolutely and unconditionally true, even though it is a dream. Life is the absolute as an affect.

If every force is an affect, does it follow that every affect is a force? The affect is, first of all, not a specific affect; instead, it is life itself in its phenomenological substance, which is irreducible to the world. It is the auto-affection, the self-impression, the primordial suffering of life driven back to itself, crushed up against itself, and overwhelmed by its own weight. Life does not affect itself in the way that the world affects it. It is not an affection at a distance, isolated, and separate, something one can escape, for example, by moving away or by turning the regard away. The affect is life affecting itself by this endogenous, internal, and constant affection, which one cannot escape in any way. When the suffering of life can no longer be supported and becomes an unbearable suffering, this experience gives birth to life's movement to take flight from itself, and as this is not possible, to change itself. It thus has need and drive. Profoundly, Freud says that "the ego remains defenseless against the excitations of the impulses."[6] Life's defenselessness against itself is even what makes the impulse. In this way, the affect is in itself a force; it continually gives rise to force within itself in virtue of what it is.

Schematically, we have just spoken about what it is to be living and consequently about the nature of the relations between the living in a community inasmuch as the nature of their relations is equally their own nature. These relations are not situated primarily in the world and its representation, putting the laws of this representation and the laws of consciousness into play. Instead, these relations are situated in life, putting the laws of life and its nature into play. In the first place, these are the affects and the forces that life produces. Hence, we can say that every community is essentially affective and based on drives. This holds not only for the fundamental communities of society—the couple and the family—but also for every community in general, whatever its interests and explicit motivations may be.

Is this conception of community not reductive? Once again, is not every concrete sociality built in and through the world? If we remember Freud's discussion of the young woman who decides to leave and to go out into the street, or the young woman who, at the beginning of Cesare Pavese's *The Fine Summer*, does the same and crosses through the space that opens up before her, should we not maintain instead that the community toward which they are going already exists within them? Would this be like the weight of an uneasiness that propels them to do what they do, like the force of this affect? Community is an *a priori*.

But is it not in the world that community is brought about, that the encounter takes place, or that the couple becomes a pair? How can the powers of representation be excluded here? Do not lovers seek some sort of mutual exhibition in the light of the world? Do they not want to see one another and to touch one another? What do they want to touch? They want to touch the other's sensation and the other's life. But, this never happens. For, if I experienced the other's pleasure in the way the other experiences it, which is to say as this pleasure is experienced, then I would be the other or the other would be me. So when the drive has become desire, one must affirm that this desire of the other in a radical sense is without an object, which is to say, there is no object for it. It wanders through the world like a ghost, because it is tied to images.

What, then, really happens in erotic pairing? The caress follows the trail of the other's pleasure. It calls upon the other's pleasure but what it touches is the other's body-object. It does not touch the other's original body, which is radically subjective and radically immanent; it does not touch the other's pleasure in itself, which is outside the world, indeed outside of every possible world. This is why the moment of intimate union and amorous fusion is paradoxically the moment in which the lovers watch out for signs, scrutinize indications, and send signals. Onto the mere arrival of pleasure, erotic behavior instinctively adds a projection of where its arrival would be for the other as for oneself. But this projection attests to its own failure in light of the fact that the other's pleasure is not presented in oneself but is co-presented. That is to say that it is appresented through the associative pairing that the real pairing imitates. But the stronger and more unifying the associative pairing is, the more evident the appresentation will be. That is to say, the more evident will be the alterity growing in it and opening up the abyss that forever separates the two places, namely, the one where the pleasure is pleasure and the one where it is presumed to be so. It is in and through this abyss that the other is the other.

Have we not rejoined the Husserlian description here? And with this description are we not once again in a phenomenology of perception that is a metaphysics of representation? In a final effort of thought, one must continue to think community in what is its ownmost, that is, in life. In life there are the living, those who are living through the ipseity and auto-affection of life. It is the nature of the auto-affection of life that needs to be made more precise. To be auto-affected does not mean, as it does in the Kantian conception or in Heidegger's commentary on it, to be the origin of its own affection and thus to posit oneself in being, taking the opposing position from the internal sense of time by converting the "I think" into an "I am." When these presuppositions of German idealism were applied to the individual, as was the case with Stirner, they led to the mythical concept of an individual who creates itself at each instant. The individual would create itself inasmuch as it both thinks and is in the same stroke.

We are saying precisely the opposite. We are saying that this experience of the self as living emerges each time in life and its auto-affection. The living being is thrown into life, inasmuch as life, by throwing itself into life, throws the living being into life. As an indication of what is to be thought here, we can borrow the words of Kierkegaard: "The I is the relation to itself as posited by an other." We can adopt these words, if we understand that this relation to oneself designates the absence of any relation, if the other is in the first place nothing posited or thought of as other, and if the other is nothing that goes beyond what emerges within this relation to oneself. The ground on which I stand is never larger than the two feet that cover it. That is the mystery of life: the living being is coextensive with all of the life within it; everything within it is its own life. The living being is not founded on itself; instead, it has a basis in life. This basis, however, is not different from itself; it is the auto-affection in which it auto-affects itself and thus with which it is identical.

These propositions should not be taken speculatively but phenomenologically. The unposited relation to oneself is the affect in its affectivity and in its radical passivity toward itself, inasmuch as it is overflowed and submerged in its own being. That is precisely what every feeling is. It is what experiences itself as overflowed by itself and, first of all, by the simple fact of experiencing oneself, that is, by life. Thus, what the members of the community have in common is the arrival of life in oneself through which each one of them enters into the self as this particular self who one is. So they are at the same time selves in the immediacy of life and others in that this experience of life is each time irreducibly in one of them.

If one must say a word here about the experience of the other, how is each one of the members of the community related to the others in life, prior to being related in a world? This primal experience is barely conceivable, because it escapes every thought. Here the living being is neither for itself nor for the other; it is only a pure experience, without a subject, without a horizon, without a meaning, and without an object. It experiences both itself—the basis (*fond*) of life—and the other, inasmuch as the other likewise has this basis. It thus does experience the other in itself but on this basis, in terms of the other's own experience of this basis. Both the self and the other have a basis in this experience. But neither the self nor the other represents it to themselves. The community is a subterranean affective layer. Each one drinks the same water from this source and this wellspring, which it itself is. But, each one does so without knowledge and without distinguishing between the self, the other, and the basis.

When, instead of being carried out "unconsciously" as a pure affect in the immediacy of life, the relation between the living occurs through the mediation of the world, when the living look at one another, represent one another, and conceive one another as egos or alter egos, a new dimension of experience emerges that must be described in its own terms. This is never simply a modification or, to put it better, a superstructure of the relation between the living in life. The key features of this relation should not be understood on the basis of representation but on the basis of life. The regard, for example, is an affect, which is what enables it to be a desire. At any rate, that is why it regards what it does regard, seeking without fail to see what it wants to see. In seeing, there is always a nonseeing and thus something unseen that altogether determines it.

Naturally, the essence of community is not something that is; instead, it is that which (*cela*)—not being a that (*ça*)—occurs as the relentless arrival of life into oneself and thus the arrival of each one into itself. This arrival occurs in many ways, yet always in conformity with laws. For example, it is not first carried out in the future but only on the basis of immediacy, and consequently, as a matter of drives and affects.

Inasmuch as the essence of community is affectivity, the community is not limited to humans alone. It includes everything that is defined in itself by the primal suffering of life and thus by the possibility of suffering. We can suffer with everything that suffers. This pathos-with is the broadest form of every conceivable community.

This pathetic community does not exclude the world but only the abstract world, which is to say, the world that does not exist and has put subjectivity out of play. But community does include the real world—the cosmos—for which every element—form, color, and so forth—exists ultimately as auto-affective. That is to say, it exists in and through this pathetic community. "The world," Kandinsky says, "sounds. It is a cosmos of spiritually affective beings. Thus, dead matter is living spirit."[7] This is why painting, for example, is not the figure of external things but the expression of their internal reality, their tonality, or what Kandinsky calls their "inner sound," an experience of forces and affects. In the end, there is only one single community, situated in this place that we have sought to delineate. There is only one single sphere of intelligibility where everything is intelligible to others and to oneself on the basis of the primal intelligibility of pathos.

Communities are multiple. The study of them is indispensable if one treats each one of them as being a variation of the *eidos* of community, a variation that would allow hitherto unperceived features to be conferred to this essence. Such a study, of course, was not possible within the limited confines of this discussion. I have sought to show only the presuppositions through which the investigations to be pursued in this vast domain will be capable of encountering the fundamental questions.

Notes

Notes to Translator's Preface

1. The best available sources of biographical information are "Vivre avec Michel Henry: Entretien avec Anne Henry," in *Auto-Donation: Entretiens et conferences*, ed. Magali Uhl (Paris: Beauchesne, 2004), 237–267; and "Un philosophe parle de sa vie (Entretien avec Roland Vaschalde)," in *Entretiens* (Arles: Sulliver, 2005), 11–21. Another source of information on Henry's life and work is the very informative Web site www.michelhenry.com.

2. Henry, *Entretiens*, 11.

3. Michel Henry, *Philosophy and Phenomenology of the Body*, trans. Girard Etzkorn (The Hague: Nijhoff, 1975).

4. Michel Henry, *The Essence of Manifestation*, trans. Girard Etzkorn (The Hague: Nijhoff, 1973).

5. Ibid., 685.

6. Jean-Luc Marion, *Reduction and Givenness*, trans. Thomas A. Carlson (Evanston, IL: Northwestern University Press, 1998), xi.

7. Michel Henry, "Quatre principes de la phénoménologie," *Revue de Métaphysique et de Morale* 1 (1991): 3–26.

8. Michel Henry, *Incarnation: Une philosophie de la chair* (Paris: Seuil, 2000).

Notes to Introduction

1. On this point, one can follow Didier Franck's remarkable analysis, which shows that when it confronts the problem of life, Heideggerianism is unable to account for life on the basis of its ontological categories. This occurs, we might

add, even though the life that it examines is only a biological life. Didier Franck, "Being and Aliveness," *Topoi* 7 (September 1988): 133–140.

2. Jean-Luc Marion, *Archives de philosophie* 51 (1988): 19.

3. Trans.: See Michel Henry, *I Am the Truth: Toward a Philosophy of Christianity*, trans. Susan Emmanuel (Stanford, Calif.: Stanford University Press, 2003).

Notes to Chapter 1: Hyletic Phenomenology and Material Phenomenology

1. Trans.: Henry uses consistently the Greek term *hyle*, which is typically translated into English as "matter." The Greek term, when used, has been retained in the translation.

2. Trans.: Henry occasionally uses the Greek term *morphe*, which means form. The Greek term, when used, has been retained in the translation.

3. Trans.: Husserl's term is *Erlebnis*. The French rendering of this term is *vécu*, which sometimes fits the English term "lived experience." I have opted to follow the terminology of the English translation, "mental process," to conform to the passages cited. While this gives more fluidity to the translation, one should note, however, that this decision obscures the terminological connection to the idea of life, contained both in the German *Erlebnis* and the French *vécu*.

4. Trans.: The Greek term *arche* has various meanings, such as "principle," "origin," and "explanation." It is clear, in this context, that Henry equates it with the idea of the origin and that it is equivalent to the German prefix *Ur*, which is commonly used in phenomenology. The Greek root, when used, has been retained throughout this translation.

5. Denise Souche-Dagues has rightly indicated this influence of the Third Logical Investigation on the argument of the *Lessons*. See *Le développement de l'intentionalité dans la phénoménologie husserlienne* (The Hague: Martinus Nijhoff, 1972), 217–218.

6. The beginning of §12 attempts to draw a strict dividing line between even a weakened sensation—for example, in its resonance—and the primary memory of this sensation.

Notes to Chapter 2: The Phenomenological Method

1. Heidegger writes, "The expression 'phenomenology' signifies primarily a concept of method" (SZ 27/31).

2. Edmund Husserl, *Formal and Transcendental Logic*, trans. Dorion Cairns (The Hague: Martinus Nijhoff, 1969) (Hua XVII 142/159).

3. Husserl writes: "[The critique of knowledge] must begin with some knowledge that it does not take unexamined from other sources, but rather provides for itself and posits as primary" (Hua II 29/23).

4. Descartes, *Principles*, in *Philosophical Writings of Descartes*, trans. John Cottingham et al. (Cambridge: Cambridge University Press, 1984).

5. Here one finds the same claim as in the later work. On this point, see my "Philosophie et subjectivité," in *Encyclopédie philosophique universelle* (Paris: Presses Universitaires de France, 1989), 1:46ff.

6. And again, Husserl asks: "How far does self-givenness extend? Is it confined to the givenness of the *cogitatio* and the ideations that grasp it in its generality? As far as self-givenness extends, so far extends our phenomenological sphere, the sphere of absolute clarity, of immanence in the genuine sense" (Hua II 10).

7. Martin Heidegger, *Four Seminars*, trans. Andrew Mitchell and François Raffoul (Bloomington: Indiana University Press, 2003).

8. In *Principles* I.46, Descartes observes, "When, for example, a severe pain is felt, the perception of this pain may be very clear, and yet for all that not distinct, because it is usually confused by the sufferers with the obscure judgment that they form upon its nature, assuming as they do that something exists in the part affected, similar to the sensation of pain of which they are alone clearly conscious."

9. See Mikkel Borch-Jacobsen, *Lacan: The Absolute Master*, trans. Douglas Brick (Stanford: Stanford University Press, 1991).

10. See my two volumes on Marx: *Marx I: Une philosophie de la réalité*, and *Marx II: Une philosophie de l'économie* (Paris: Gallimard, 1976).

Notes to Chapter 3: Pathos-With

1. On the reason for this situation where, in the process of its explication, the being of the ego does not escape "in large part" (*im weitem Ausmaße*) but completely from the acts of perception, and on the necessity of replacing this content, which conceals itself from being perceived through formal, empty, and transcendent structures, see the preceding study on "The Phenomenological Method."

2. On this point, see my *Philosophie et phénoménologie du corps* (Paris: Presses Universitaires de France, 1988).

3. Didier Franck, *Chair et corps: Sur la phénoménologie de Husserl* (Paris: Minuit, 1981), 152 ff.

4. Max Scheler, *The Nature of Sympathy*, trans. Peter Heath (Hamden, CT: Archon Books: 1970).

5. Mikkel Borch-Jacobsen, "Hypnosis in Psychoanalysis," *Representations* 27 (1989): 92–110.

6. Sigmund Freud, *Gesammelte Werke* (London: Imago, 1940), 10:212.

7. Wassily Kandinsky, "On the Question of Form," in *Kandinsky: Complete Writings on Art*, ed. Kenneth C. Lindsay and Peter Vergo (Boston: G. K. Hall, 1982), 2:250.

Perspectives in Continental Philosophy Series
John D. Caputo, series editor

1. John D. Caputo, ed., *Deconstruction in a Nutshell: A Conversation with Jacques Derrida.*
2. Michael Strawser, *Both/And: Reading Kierkegaard—From Irony to Edification.*
3. Michael D. Barber, *Ethical Hermeneutics: Rationality in Enrique Dussel's Philosophy of Liberation.*
4. James H. Olthuis, ed., *Knowing* Other-*wise: Philosophy at the Threshold of Spirituality.*
5. James Swindal, *Reflection Revisited: Jürgen Habermas's Discursive Theory of Truth.*
6. Richard Kearney, *Poetics of Imagining: Modern and Postmodern.* Second edition.
7. Thomas W. Busch, *Circulating Being: From Embodiment to Incorporation—Essays on Late Existentialism.*
8. Edith Wyschogrod, *Emmanuel Levinas: The Problem of Ethical Metaphysics.* Second edition.
9. Francis J. Ambrosio, ed., *The Question of Christian Philosophy Today.*
10. Jeffrey Bloechl, ed., *The Face of the Other and the Trace of God: Essays on the Philosophy of Emmanuel Levinas.*
11. Ilse N. Bulhof and Laurens ten Kate, eds., *Flight of the Gods: Philosophical Perspectives on Negative Theology.*
12. Trish Glazebrook, *Heidegger's Philosophy of Science.*
13. Kevin Hart, *The Trespass of the Sign: Deconstruction, Theology, and Philosophy.*

14. Mark C. Taylor, *Journeys to Selfhood: Hegel and Kierkegaard*. Second edition.

15. Dominique Janicaud, Jean-François Courtine, Jean-Louis Chrétien, Michel Henry, Jean-Luc Marion, and Paul Ricoeur, *Phenomenology and the "Theological Turn": The French Debate*.

16. Karl Jaspers, *The Question of German Guilt*. Introduction by Joseph W. Koterski, S.J.

17. Jean-Luc Marion, *The Idol and Distance: Five Studies*. Translated with an introduction by Thomas A. Carlson.

18. Jeffrey Dudiak, *The Intrigue of Ethics: A Reading of the Idea of Discourse in the Thought of Emmanuel Levinas*.

19. Robyn Horner, *Rethinking God as Gift: Marion, Derrida, and the Limits of Phenomenology*.

20. Mark Dooley, *The Politics of Exodus: Søren Kierkegaard's Ethics of Responsibility*.

21. Merold Westphal, Overcoming Onto-Theology: *Toward a Postmodern Christian Faith*.

22. Edith Wyschogrod, Jean-Joseph Goux and Eric Boynton, eds., *The Enigma of Gift and Sacrifice*.

23. Stanislas Breton, *The Word and the Cross*. Translated with an introduction by Jacquelyn Porter.

24. Jean-Luc Marion, *Prolegomena to Charity*. Translated by Stephen E. Lewis.

25. Peter H. Spader, *Scheler's Ethical Personalism: Its Logic, Development, and Promise*.

26. Jean-Louis Chrétien, *The Unforgettable and the Unhoped For*. Translated by Jeffrey Bloechl.

27. Don Cupitt, *Is Nothing Sacred? The Non-Realist Philosophy of Religion: Selected Essays*.

28. Jean-Luc Marion, *In Excess: Studies of Saturated Phenomena*. Translated by Robyn Horner and Vincent Berraud.

29. Phillip Goodchild, ed., *Rethinking Philosophy of Religion: Approaches from Continental Philosophy*.

30. William J. Richardson, S.J., *Heidegger: Through Phenomenology to Thought*.

31. Jeffrey Andrew Barash, *Martin Heidegger and the Problem of Historical Meaning*.

32. Jean-Louis Chrétien, *Hand to Hand: Listening to the Work of Art*. Translated by Stephen E. Lewis.

33. Jean-Louis Chrétien, *The Call and the Response*. Translated with an introduction by Anne Davenport.

34. D. C. Schindler, *Han Urs von Balthasar and the Dramatic Structure of Truth: A Philosophical Investigation*.

35. Julian Wolfreys, ed., *Thinking Difference: Critics in Conversation*.

36. Allen Scult, *Being Jewish/Reading Heidegger: An Ontological Encounter*.

37. Richard Kearney, *Debates in Continental Philosophy: Conversations with Contemporary Thinkers*.

38. Jennifer Anna Gosetti-Ferencei, *Heidegger, Hölderlin, and the Subject of Poetic Language: Towards a New Poetics of Dasein*.

39. Jolita Pons, *Stealing a Gift: Kierkegaard's Pseudonyms and the Bible*.

40. Jean-Yves Lacoste, *Experience and the Absolute: Disputed Questions on the Humanity of Man*. Translated by Mark Raftery-Skehan.

41. Charles P. Bigger, *Between Chora and the Good: Metaphor's Metaphysical Neighborhood*.

42. Dominique Janicaud, *Phenomenology "Wide Open": After the French Debate*. Translated by Charles N. Cabral.

43. Ian Leask and Eoin Cassidy, eds. *Givenness and God: Questions of Jean-Luc Marion*.

44. Jacques Derrida, *Sovereignties in Question: The Poetics of Paul Celan*. Edited by Thomas Dutoit and Outi Pasanen.

45. William Desmond, *Is There a Sabbath for Thought? Between Religion and Philosophy*.

46. Bruce Ellis Benson and Norman Wirzba, eds. *The Phenomenology of Prayer*.

47. S. Clark Buckner and Matthew Statler, eds. *Styles of Piety: Practicing Philosophy after the Death of God*.

48. Kevin Hart and Barbara Wall, eds. *The Experience of God: A Postmodern Response*.

49. John Panteleimon Manoussakis, *After God: Richard Kearney and the Religious Turn in Continental Philosophy*.

50. John Martis, *Philippe Lacoue-Labarthe: Representation and the Loss of the Subject*.

51. Jean-Luc Nancy, *The Ground of the Image*. Translated by Jeff Fort.

52. Edith Wyschogrod, *Crossover Queries: Dwelling with Negatives, Embodying Philosophy's Others*.

53. Gerald Bruns, *On the Anarchy of Poetry and Philosophy: A Guide for the Unruly*.

54. Brian Treanor, *Aspects of Alterity: Levinas, Marcel, and the Contemporary Debate*.

55. Simon Mogan Wortham, *Counter-Institutions: Jacques Derrida and the Question of the University*.

56. Leonard Lawlor, *The Implications of Immanence: Toward a New Concept of Life*.

57. Clayton Crockett, *Interstices of the Sublime: Theology and Psychoanalytic Theory*.

58. Bettina Bergo, Joseph Cohen, and Raphael Zagury-Orly, eds., *Judeities: Questions for Jacques Derrida*. Translated by Bettina Bergo, and Michael B. Smith.

59. Jean-Luc Marion, *On the Ego and on God: Further Cartesian Questions*. Translated by Christina M. Gschwandtner.

60. Jean-Luc Nancy, *Philosophical Chronicles*. Translated by Franson Manjali.

61. Jean-Luc Nancy, *Dis-Enclosure: The Deconstruction of Christianity*. Translated by Bettina Bergo, Gabriel Malenfant, and Michael B. Smith.

62. Andrea Hurst, *Derrida Vis-à-vis Lacan: Interweaving Deconstruction and Psychoanalysis*.

63. Jean-Luc Nancy, *Noli me tangere: On the Raising of the Body*. Translated by Sarah Clift, Pascale-Anne Brault, and Michael Naas.

64. Jacques Derrida, *The Animal That Therefore I Am*. Edited by Marie-Louise Mallet, Translated by David Wills.

65. Jean-Luc Marion, *The Visible and the Revealed*. Translated by Christina M. Gschwandtner and others.

www.ingramcontent.com/pod-product-compliance
Lightning Source LLC
Chambersburg PA
CBHW031251290426
44109CB00012B/530